CLASSIC BOULDER CLIMBS

By
Fred Knapp and Michael Stevens

available from

Sharp End
Publishing

P.O. Box 1613
Boulder, CO 80306
inforock@aol.com

CLASSIC BOULDER CLIMBS

by Fred Knapp & Mike Stevens

ISBN 0-9657079-7-0

Library of Congress Catalog Number 98-090117

READ THIS BEFORE USING THIS GUIDE

DANGER

WARNING:

Rock climbing is a dangerous activity. Participation in this sport could result in injury or death.

Do not rely on information in this book for your personal safety. Your safety depends on your judgment, experience, and a realistic assessment of your ability. If you have any doubts, do not attempt a climb. Do not treat this guide as an instruction manual or a bible.

Verify ratings and information for yourself. The information in this book may be inaccurate. Fixed hardware and rock change over time. Ratings are subjective. Information is gathered from a variety of sources and may be incorrect. Don't believe any ratings in this guide.

THE AUTHORS AND PUBLISHER EXPRESSLY DISCLAIM ALL REPRESENTATIONS AND WARRANTIES REGARDING THIS GUIDE, THE ACCURACY OF THE INFORMATION HEREIN, AND THE RESULTS OF YOUR USE HEREOF, INCLUDING WITHOUT LIMITATION, IMPLIED WARRANTIES OF MERCHANTABILITY AND FITNESS FOR A PARTICULAR PURPOSE. THE USER ASSUMES ALL RISK ASSOCIATED WITH THE USE OF THIS GUIDE.

If you do not accept full responsibility for your own actions, do not use this guide. Climbing is inherently dangerous. You will probably get hurt or die.

TABLE OF CONTENTS

Boulder Overview Map 5
Introduction 7
Boulder Canyon 11
    Elephant Buttresses 14
    The Dome 17
    Brick Wall 18
    Cob Rock 19
    Happy Hour 20
    Security Risk 22
    Practice Rock 26
    Bell Buttress 27
    The Boulderado 29
    Animal World 30
    Coney Island 32
    Easter Rock 33
    Castle Rock 35
The Flatirons 39
    First Faltiron 42
    Third Flatiron 44
    Dinosaur Mt./Bear Canyon 47
    Fern Canyon 63
    The Maiden 76
Eldorado Canyon 81
    Wind Tower 86
    Whale's Tail 89
    Redgarden Wall 91
    West Ridge 111
    The Bastille 114
    Supremacy Rock 122
Bouldering Areas 124
Index 127

GEAR FOR THE VERTICAL WORLD

Neptune Mountaineering

Table Mesa Shopping Center, Boulder (303) 499-8866
Open Weekdays 10am - 8pm, Weekends 10am - 6pm

barbara cantor on the crux of the owl, photo mark cantor

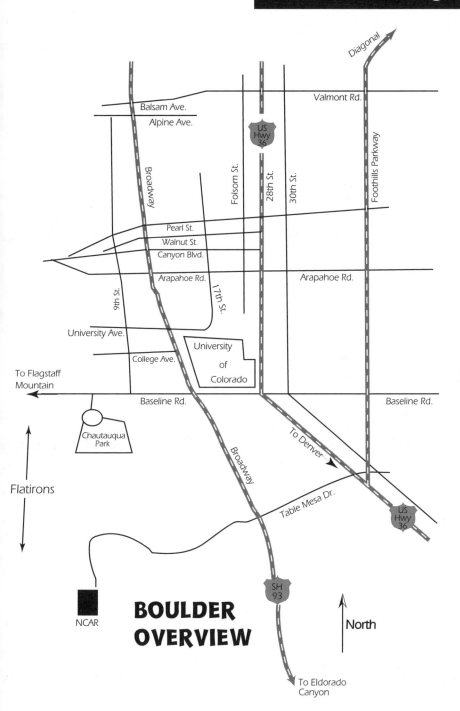

BOULDER
OVERVIEW

PLANET BOULDER

By Michael Stevens

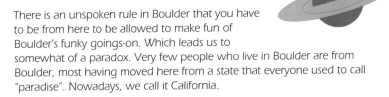

There is an unspoken rule in Boulder that you have to be from here to be allowed to make fun of Boulder's funky goings-on. Which leads us to somewhat of a paradox. Very few people who live in Boulder are from Boulder, most having moved here from a state that everyone used to call "paradise". Nowadays, we call it California.

I self am a Colorado native, but not even I am from Boulder. I grew up about 45 minutes out of Boulder, but have lived here for a dozen years, so I am considered to be "from here". As a rule, I don't make fun of Boulder. Lots of strange stuff goes on here, and you'll just have to take my word for it when I say that your visit just won't be complete without sampling at least a couple of the following Boulder activities on a rest day:

1. Spend an afternoon on the Pearl Street Mall. Don't ask why, just do it. Located downtown, Pearl Street is a large open air mall that attracts every walk of life. Just go and watch people, although there's a good chance that you'll be watched just as much. Good for nightlife as well with hot spots being The Rio (great margaritas), The Oasis and The Walnut Brewery micobreweries.

2. Visit the National Center for Atmospheric Research. This place is located high above Boulder, and can be reached by driving west on Table Mesa Drive until the road stops. Lots of stuff goes on here that I don't fully understand, but they have a great visitor center, and the views of some of the Flatirons are great. When you're done atmosphering, go on a hike up into those very same Flatirons. Several trails leave from the NCAR parking lot.

3. Walk the University of Colorado campus. When I was a student here, we had lots of nice open space and grass. Lately pavement and parking garages seem to be in vogue, but it's still one of the prettiest campuses in the country. I have no reason to lie. My degree hasn't really gotten my anywhere...yet.

4. Stroll up "The Hill" This is the University district of Boulder, and is located just west of campus from University Blvd. to Euclid Ave. Most of the action takes place in a three block stretch. In addition to the most coffee shops possible in such a short distance there are lots of restaurants, shops, and hippies, hippies and hippies looking for spare change. To have a really fulfilling trip, get a nipple pierced at K&K Jewelry on the corner of College and 13th.

5. Hang out at the Boulder Reservoir. Take the Diagonal (Hwy 119) north out of the city, then turn left of Jay Road. Follow the signs from there. It's a couple of bucks to get in, but it's usually worth it. Sunning, swimming, lots of colorful locals, tattooed women, and as occasional rousing game of coed naked volleyball is played on the beach.

Have Fun!

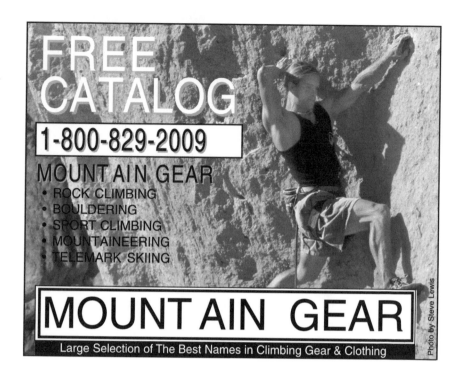
ICONS FOR QUICK REFERENCE

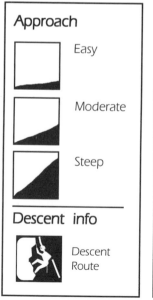

Approach

Easy

Moderate

Steep

Descent info

Descent Route

Route Type

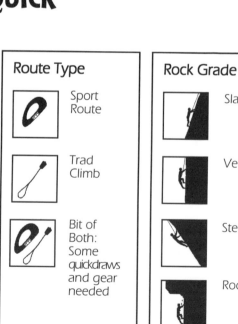

Sport Route

Trad Climb

Bit of Both: Some quickdraws and gear needed

Rock Grade

Slab

Vertical

Steep

Roof

BOULDER CANYON

Jane Sears on Country Club Crack
Photo by Dan Hare

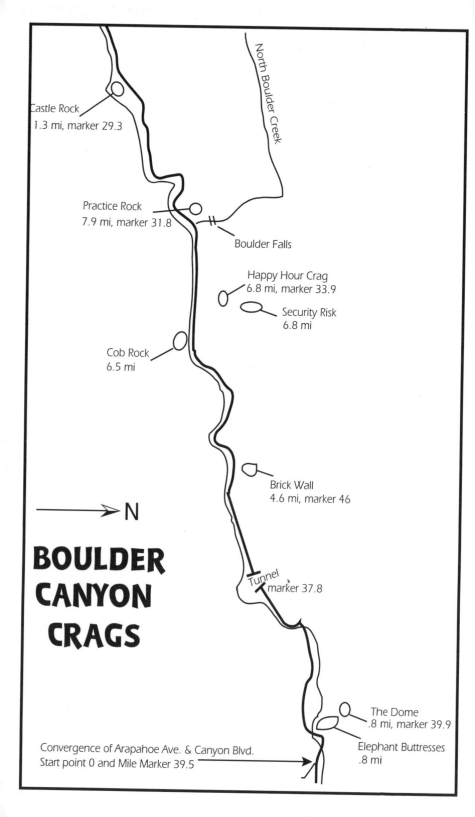

Castle Rock
1.3 mi, marker 29.3

North Boulder Creek

Practice Rock
7.9 mi, marker 31.8

Boulder Falls

Happy Hour Crag
6.8 mi, marker 33.9

Security Risk
6.8 mi

Cob Rock
6.5 mi

Brick Wall
4.6 mi, marker 46

⟶ N

BOULDER
CANYON
CRAGS

Tunnel
marker 37.8

The Dome
.8 mi, marker 39.9

Elephant Buttresses
.8 mi

Convergence of Arapahoe Ave. & Canyon Blvd.
Start point 0 and Mile Marker 39.5 ⟶

BOULDER CANYON

Boulder Canyon offers a great combination of classic lines and newer sport crags. With access provided via a two lane highway, approaches are limited, for the most part, to a 10-15 minute walk. Some of the crags lie just 20 feet from the highway!

To get to Boulder Canyon, take Canyon Blvd. west out of Boulder (See Boulder map). Reset your trip meter where Arapahoe Ave. comes in from the left and intersects Canyon Blvd. (at the bridge on the left). All mileages to the crags are referenced from this point.

The main obstacle to be aware of is North Boulder Creek. Many of the crags are located on the "other" side of the creek, and one may have to ford this to reach a particular destination. In the case of some of the crags, a bridge, stepping stone path, or Tyrolean traverse, leads the way. For others, just roll up those pants and wade across. PLEASE BEWARE! NORTH BOULDER CREEK CAN RUN VERY HIGH AND FAST, PARTICULARLY IN LATE SPRING AND EARLY SUMMER (MAY-MID JULY). CROSSING WITHOUT BENEFIT OF A BRIDGE DURING THESE TIMES IS STRONGLY DISCOURAGED.

ELEPHANT BUTTRESSES

The Elephant Buttresses are the first crags encountered in Boulder Canyon. There are pullouts on both sides of the road at mile marker 0.8. Park here, walk north, and cross the bridge. Follow a trail along Boulder Creek until a climbing access sign points to a steep trail. Follow this for about 100 yards to its intersection with a small steam. A path on the stream's uphill side takes one to a water pipe. Head south along the water pipe (be very careful walking along this— a slip could produce quite a fall in some areas!) until the base of the buttresses is reached. Beware of poison ivy in the summer months.

The buttresses are numbered one through four, with the northernmost buttress being number one, the southernmost number four.

To descend, scramble down the obvious gullies just north of the buttresses. The steep gully between the second and third buttresses does not make a good descent.

First Buttress

2nd Buttress-left side

1. Flash Dihedral 5.8+

Begin on a broken pile 50 ft. above the water pipe, and follow the shallow dihedral on the NW face.

2. Tough Situation 5.9

Approach by scrambling up the easy broken gully to a good belay stance just below the angular summit block. Attack the roof and left-facing dihedral.

3. Classic Finger Crack 5.9

Same belay stance as above. Take the obvious stellar finger crack up the face of the summit block.

4. Pine Tree Route 5.4 - 5.5

Ascend the varied face directly below the tree. 60m rope recommended.

5. Wingtip 5.10c/d

Begin 75 feet up the gully under a shallow roof. Turn it (.9) then take the overhanging left-facing corner. Gain a nice ledge, then finish over easier ground.

2nd & 3rd Buttresses

6. Left Wing 5.10b/c

Begin 75 feet up the gully on a ledge. Take the leaning left-facing dihedral, then break left past two bolts. Keep heading left where the route roofs out, then turn the final roof near the top. Gain the ledge mentioned above, and finish on easy ground.

7. What's Up? 5.10a/b

Same start as for *Left Wing*, lieback around square roof to a belay. Continue straight up the line above roof.

8. FM 5.11c

Awesome climb up a steep, left-facing dihedral. Start up the gully from the pipe and climb into an A-shaped roof. Move up and left into corner.

9. Standard Route 5.7

Climb begins from the water pipe right of the gully. Go up the left-facing corner to a large ramp. Belay at its top. Continue right up the overhanging wall (.7) or straight up (.9). A final pitch moves left up the obvious weakness.

10. Monster Woman 5.8+

Variation of the above. Begin to right of *Standard* at eye bolt, move up and left passing the roof.

11. Ah Maw 5.10a

Climb through the center of the roof right of Monster Woman.

12. Zolar Czakl 5.10a
Begin up a flake in the back of the cave, head right a bit, then straight up over 5.9 terrain to the top.

13. Northwest Face 5.8+
Begin level with where the pipe heads into the cave, and traverse right over 3rd class terrain. Follow a line up and slightly left, picking up a broken left-facing corner halfway up.

14. The Heartland 5.9+
Begin as for 13, but keep traversing right. Climb into a difficult thin crack which terminates at a broken ledge. Pick up another thin crack left of the very large dihedral and follow it to the top.

The best descent is to make the longish walk to the easy gully north of the second buttress.

The Dome

Approach as for the Elephant Buttresses. Cross the bridge and follow access signs up to the aqueduct, then pick a trail which heads to the clean granite dome.

Head east to the gully between the Elephant Buttresses and The Dome.

1. East Slabs 5.5

This 2- pitch route contains a little of everything—cracks, face and a roof. Begin on the right side of The Dome, about 100' up from the bottom of the face. Climb a shallow right-facing corner (5.5) or start up a section of broken flakes (5.4) 8' further uphill. Either way, aim for the obvious crack on the smooth slab above. Follow this crack for 40 feet (gear up to 3.5" is nice), then friction up (crux), aiming for a belay alcove. Be prepared to run it out a tad on the slab. Belay on good gear in the alcove. A short 25' pitch leads over a small roof to a pine tree belay.

2. Cozyhang 5.7

Another classic moderate, however beware of almost unavoidable rope drag and communication problems at times. Still if you're at the crag, don't miss it.

Begin about 70 feet up and right from the base of The Dome noted by 3 small roofs crossing the lower face. Climb the slab below the roofs, place gear, then turn the roofs via some deceptively difficult moves on polished granite (.7).

Find a crack that angles up and left towards the massive roof block at mid-face and follow it up under the roof. Belay, and get some rope signals ready.

Next, head left and down a bit and aim for the left side of the roof. Climb up the left side of the roof, cut right up a slab and set up a belay under a large A-shaped roof. The last pitch climbs straight through the A-roof and then up the clean slab to the top. * See topo for 2nd and 3rd pitch variation.

3. The Owl 5.7

The route goes straight up the middle of The Dome's face. Start at the low point on the face, cruise a fourth class buttress, and angle up and left to a ramp with shallow cracks. Break towards a little roof above the ramp, and turn it on the right. Cross a short slab, then work into an obtuse left-facing corner. Reach around the bulge to a huge chickenhead.

Head straight up a steep crack directly across from the huge roof, step left at the top and belay. Cross a slab up and right to 2nd *Cozyhang* belay. Finish on this route.

Brick Wall

anchors

The routes on this granite buttress have been led at one time or another, but due to the sketchiness of the leads these routes are regarded mostly as topropes.

1. The Perfect Route   5.10c
The bottom left part of the face forms a bowl. Climb straight up the middle of this, then bear left below a small A-shaped roof. Continue up the left side of the face

2. Living on the Edge   5.11b/c
Begin as for #1, but tackle the small roof straight on. From here, continue up the difficult prow to the bulge and the top.

3. The South Face   5.10b
Begin on the right side of the lower slab and climb straight up to a horizontal fracture. Head left here, then cruise straight up and out the bulge.

Scramble to the top from the right-side, being careful not to dislodge loose rocks onto the road. Back up the old bolts at the anchor!

Cob Rock

Cob Rock is one of Boulder Canyon's most popular destinations for multi-pitch climbs. It lies on the southern side of the canyon, and isn't a great place to go when it's cold, but is perfect for hot summer days. A Tyrolean traverse facilitates a creek crossing during high water.

1. Night Vision 5.10b

A fine route that begins on the left side of the lower pedestal. Climb past two bolts to a belay on a small ledge. Next, climb the arete past two more bolts, supplemented by gear. Always bolting on the sly, the unstoppable Dan Hare drilled these bolts in the dark on the lead, thus the name.

2. East Crack 5.10a/b

Lies to the right of *Night Vision* after the first pitch. From there the goal is to move right above the roof to gain a thin crack, which leads to a belay ledge. Head up a 5.7 crack on the right to the top.

3. Houston's Crack 5.7

Scary offwidth that is harder than the old-school grade implies.

4. Aid Crack 5.10d

A creatively named aid crack up the center of the low buttress.

5. Face Route 5.11a R

A scary excursion with another witty name. *Face Route* is somewhat tricky to protect and is usually toproped.

6. Empor 5.7+

An old classic route that might feel harder than its traditional rating. Begin on the north face at a big boulder, scramble up to some difficult face moves (crux) that lead left into a right-facing corner. Belay at the top of the corner in a convenient slot.

Descend by heading south off the summit, then down the slope on the west.

Cob Rock

NW View

HAPPY HOUR CRAG

Happy Hour Crag

Happy Hour is one of Boulder Canyon's most popular crags, probably due to the fact that nearly all of the routes can be toproped. It lies on the north side of the canyon a little over seven miles up. It can be seen from the road, and there is a pullout directly across from the approach trail. This crag receives sun all day and is home to many good routes in the 5.7- 5.10 range.

1. I, Robot   5.7
2. Are We Not Men   5.7
3. Twofers   5.8
4. Twofers Gully   5.6
5. The Big Spit   5.9
6. Rush Hour   5.10b
7. Last Call   5.9
8. Dementia   5.10a
9. Malign   5.7

10. Tipsey   5.9
Climb #9 to reach it
11. Nightcap   5.8
12. Skid Row   5.9+
13. Grins   5.9+
Up and right over a tooth
13A. Dan Hare Route   5.11d

David Levine on Dimentia. Photo by Dan Hare.

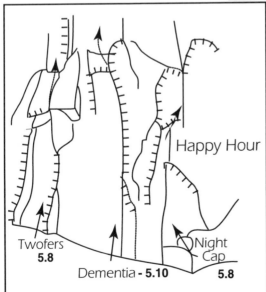

13B. Last Laugh   5.10c
Climb to the tooth on 13
and climb left past 3 bolts;
supplemental gear.
14. Hands Off   5.7
15. The Great Race   5.9+
16. Baby Aliens   5.12a
17. Bad Sneakers   5.9+
18. Cruel Shoes   5.9

Happy Hour

Twofers
5.8

Dementia - **5.10**

Night
Cap
5.8

Security Risk

Security Risk is a wonderful sport climbing crag which is usually free of the throngs down below at Happy Hour; the 25 minute hike is just 20 minutes too long for them. This crag is seeing continuous development and contains sport routes with interesting and varied moves. With afternoon sun, this crag is a great place to get a tan in the winter, However, during the summer, choose it as a morning area.

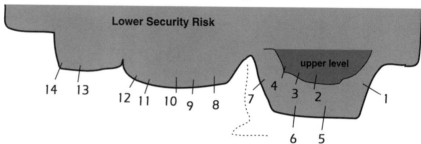

1. Enema of the People 5.11d/12a
Climb past five bolts, staying to the left of the arete to the 2-bolt anchor.

2. Comfortably Numb 5.12a
Start off the ledge above and to the right of *Enema...* Stoppers, Friends, and RP's will help you protect this climb.

3. Men are from Mars 5.11a/b
Begin from the same ledge as for #2 and ascend the bolted line which climbs to the right of a left-facing dihedral.

4. Security Risk 5.10a or 5.10d
An outstanding crack route. The short 10d first pitch begins just right of the big corner in a finger crack and follows this to the roof/corner and up to the belay. This short pitch ends at the comfortable ledge.

Alternatively, one can climb the wide crack around the corner to the right (.8) or the short corner right of that (which requires traversing back left to the 5.8 crack).

The next pitch starts up a chimney, pulls a small roof and attacks the long splitter above. A classic 5.9 pitch.

8. Central Insecurity 5.12c/d
A challenging route that meanders past 9 bolts to a 2-bolt anchor 85' up.

9. Enemy of the People 5.12b
A classic Randy Leavitt trad route that moves past two bolts to a roof then a corner.

10. Project

11. Ecstasy of the People 5.12d
Seven bolts to a 2-bolt anchor.

12. Maximum Security 5.9+
Bring plenty of stoppers to protect this route.

13. Eldo of the People 5.12a
Begin just right of *Scraping By*, protecting the first bit with Friends. Move up a bolted line which trends left to the right side of the arete. Then move back right, pull a roof and move to a 2-bolt anchor.

14. Scraping By 5.10a
Start left of the arete and climb a left-facing dihedral, utilizing mostly small and medium sized pro.

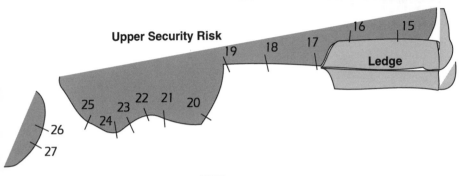

Upper Security Risk

Ledge

15. Hot Wire 5.12b/c

One of the canyon's finest routes—
100' long with 13 bolts to a 2-bolt anchor.

16. Hot Flyer 5.11d/12a
A renowned favorite of the crag, this
85' route has it all. Great climbing, thought
provoking and powerful at times. Climbs
past 9 bolts to chain anchors at the top of a
slabular finish above the roof.

17. The Juice 5.12d
Begins right of a left-facing crack and
pulls three roofs, the last being the largest.
10 bolts lead to the chain anchors 75'
above.

18. Plan B 5.12b
Stellar! You may want to stick-clip the
start. The finish has two options, or rather a
plan A and a plan B. Either end at the
Goldshut anchors 10 bolts up, or continue
2 more bolts to an anchor w/ biners.

19. Get Smart 5.10d
Bring up a wide range of gear for this
route that begins on 5.9 offwidth and
continues past a ledge up a thin crack to a
2-bolt anchor. Another pitch continues up a
right-facing dihedral (5.10d R).

20. Just a Little Insecure 5.12a
This short powerful route is best
started with a stick-clip. Ascend past three
bolts to the 2-bolt anchor.

21. Cracking the Code 5.11a
Begins behind trees around the
corner from #20. This three pitch route is
an enjoyable outing. (pitches: 11a, 10b, 9+)

22. Crossfire 5.9
A traditional line. Takes a route up
flakes, corners, and over a roof.

23. Dan's New Route 5.11c
A tricky outing that begins up a corner
and proceeds up the face to a crux mantle
move. Anchors beneath the roof.

24. Crash Test Blondes 5.11c
Begin right of a large dead tree. The
first bolt is a ways up. Climb past 7 bolts in
all to a 2-bolt anchor above the roof.

25. Pup 5.9
Begin about 20' left of *Crash*. Start left
of a small overhang. Climb left of the
overhang and move past 5 bolts on the
right side of the arete. Pull a roof and
continue straight up to a 2-bolt anchor
above a ledge.

26. Turmoil 5.11d

Harder than it looks. A tricky and
dynamic slab climb up the left side of
Higher Security Risk.

27. Cold Shot 5.11a
A balancy warm-up route found 100'
up from *Pup*. It passes 5 bolts to a chain
anchor.

UPPER SECURITY RISK

Steve Levin on Hot Wire

Practice Rock

Practice Rock, found just after the 33 mile marker going up Canyon, is a popular toprope crag with a virtually nonexistent approach (bumper belays possible). Park off the road just below the crag. The routes are most often toproped from a long sling arrangement, though the far right route is a reasonable lead.

1. Left Crack   5.9+
The obvious crack up the left side.

2. ?   5.9-
The crack just right of #1.

3. Regular Route   5.11b
The meandering crack up the middle.

4. Lieback   5.10a
The flake on the right side of the face.

Electra Glide 5.8+
About 25 yards upcanyon from Practice Rock, and accessed from the same pullout, is a clean chunk of stone called Electra Glide. The zig-zag crack up the left side is an excellent 5.8+ lead. A tree serves as the belay and rappel anchor.

The BOWLING ALLEY (A Sport Crag)
A new sport crag is located about 30 yards above and east of Practice Rock . The lowest cliff sports an easy 5.11 and a 5.8. The main tier from left to right includes an 11,12b,12c (Amazing Face—a big roof),12a (with or without the chiseled hold),12b,11c. The upper tier holds two 5.10's on the right and a 5.11 on the left side of the ledge.

Bell Buttress

Bell Buttress is the large crag directly across the road and creek from Practice Rock. A short but tricky approach crosses the river and scrambles to a horizontal ledge that crosses below the main wall. Only the most popular and best climbs are described.

1. Hound Dog 5.10d/11a
This isolated sport climb is quite popular. Soon a 5.13 version will cut left. In the meantime veer right into a groove with anchors. Eight bolts.

2. Grand Inquisitor 5.12a R
Frequently toproped from *Hound Dog's* anchors, this route isn't often led. A dyno crux is near the first bolt; then it eases on sketchy face holds and questionable protection.

3. Verve 5.13c/d
What came first the climb or the clothing? Ring bolts on the aesthetic arete.

4. Cosmosis 5.10a
Most people just do the first pitch of this summit route. Excellent stemming to an anchor.

5. West Crack 5.9+
This crack is the first obvious crack about 25 feet right of *Cosmosois*. Fixed anchors are generally in place.

6. West Face 5.9+
The righthand neighbor of the previous route. This quality crack is most often ended after one pitch, but can be taken to the summit by following a right-facing dihedral.

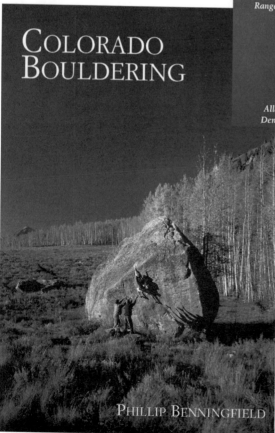

The Boulderado

This roadside crag is popular for its beginner topropes, but also houses some fun sport routes. Topropes on the left side vary from 5.5-5.8. Pick your own lines or consult *Front Range Topropes* by Fred Knapp. The right side has two sport routes, a mixed route, and a toprope.

A. Q's 5.9+
Named for an eating establishment in the Hotel Boulderado. 6 bolts/ 3 bolt-sling anchor.

B. Jazz on the Mezzanine 5.12 a/b
If you're free on the weekends, head to the Boulderado for some Jazz on the Mezzanine, with a dessert from Q's. A bouldery start leads out toward the arete. 4 bolts/ stick-clip.

C. Hell in a Bucket 5.12d
The crack right of *Jazz* can be toproped.

D. Suite 11 5.11c
This sweet 11 requires some gear to get to the two bolts.

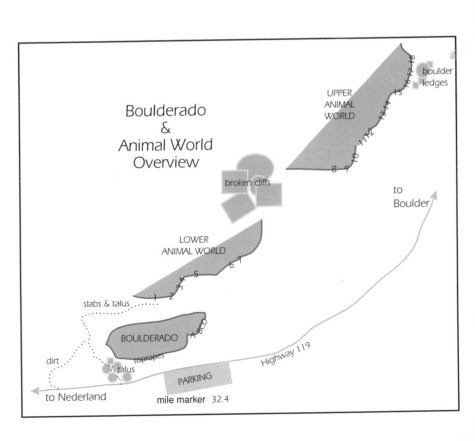

Boulderado
&
Animal World
Overview

Animal World

A relatively new crag, this is becoming one of the gems of Boulder Canyon. Home to an abundance of quality routes with various exposures, this is one of the best places to clip bolts. The trad routes aren't on par, so I haven't even mentioned them.

The approach begins on the left side of the Boulderado by either ascending big talus or further upcanyon on a mud slope. A well-defined trail leads one above the Boulderado then traverses slabs and talus to the first routes, directly above the center of the lower cliff. Cairns mark the tricky section. Refer to overview on Boulderado page for layout of the hillside.

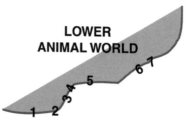

LOWER ANIMAL WORLD

UPPER ANIMAL WORLD

1. Animal Riots Activist   5.11d/12a
The first route encountered on the trail. Climb a slab to a crux bulge. Bouldery. Seven bolts and anchors.

2. Piles of Trials   5.12a/b
The neighboring route. Interesting and somewhat sustained. 5 bolts to anchors.

3. Cannibas Sportiva   5.11a
Begin up cracks to finish on a bolted line. Around the corner from *Piles*.

4. Feeding the Beast   5.12a
Climb past bolts up an arete to a belay. Continue up the left line of bolts.

4a. Joint Venture   5.11a
The righthand line of bolts above the belay.

5. Jaycee's Dance   5.8+
Nine bolts protect this great moderate route.

6. Free Willie   5.11a/b
The leftmost of two bolted routes that look as though they could have been climbed with clean protection. Seven bolts.

7. Days of Future Past   5.12a
Somewhat dirty, but bolted, crack route. Five or six bolts.

8. Hands of Destiny   5.12c
This bouldery route was originally a trad lead retro-bolted by the first ascenscionist. The crux is on the lower facet, though the upper 5.11+ slab shouldn't be taken lightly. 12 bolts on the first pitch. (An optional upper pitch climbs steep 5.10 terrain).

9. Animal Instinct   5.12b/c
The stunning arete right of *Hands...* Technical climbing with several cruxes. Clip *Sundog's* first two bolts to begin this route.

10. Sundog 5.11d
The tricky slab on the opposite side of the arete from the previous route.

11. Evolution Revolution   5.12b
The bolted route that heads through the roof crack. 8 bolts.

12. Global Gorilla 5.11b/ 5.12b/ 5.12b

This three-pitch route can be done as one extremely long pitch. Begin in a dihedral with two bolts and continue along an arete past 9 more to the first anchor (11b). For more challenge continue up a stellar arete past 5 more bolts (12b). Six more bolts lead to the final anchors (12b). Several rappels reach the ground.

13. Animal Magnetism 5.11c

One of the best bolted pitches of its grade. A crux on the lower wall leads to sustained but easier climbing through a series of left-trending arches and underclings. 13 bolts. anchors/60m rope.

14. Animal Antagonism 5.13b

Begins right of *Magnetism* and conquers the imposing wall above.

5. Kudjo Tranquilizer 5.12a

Looks can be deceiving! Begin as for the previous route but branch right onto the right wall of a dihedral. 15 bolts to a 2 bolt anchors.

16. Kudjo Magnetism 5.12a

A link-up. Climb the crux of *Kudjo Tranquilizer (first 4 bolts)*, join *Animal Antagonism* for two bolts, then work over to *Animal Magnetism*.

17. Pitbull Prowser 5.11b

Begin near a large tree and follow 12 bolts past cracks and seams to an anchor. An upper portion has yet to be freed. It is also possible to start from the boulder and traverse into the 3rd bolt, avoiding the low crux (5.10d)

18. New Beginnings 5.11c

A good route that needs a new ending. Clipping the anchors is a crux for sore fingers. 8 bolts.

Dan Hare on Pitbull Prowser

Coney Island

Coney Island lies at a turn in the road at mile marker 31.8. The cliff is easier to spot when coming down the canyon. Parking on the south side of the road is limited. Coney Island consists of two cliffs, an upper and a lower. A trail leads to the small but steep lower wall. Continue around right to the upper wall which features cracks, dihedrals, and a large shield on the left side.

Lower Cliff

1. The Bait 5.11a
The nice dihedral requires some finger-size gear. Four bolts and anchors.

2. Twist and Shout 5.13b
Steep arete with 6 bolts to anchor.

3. Flytrap 5.11c
Jugs protected by 5 bolts up right of the arete to anchors.

4. Flies in the Soup 5.11c
Steep, but only 3 bolts to anchors.

5. Prong 5.12c
Steep wall ending at *Fly Swatter.*

6. Fly Swatter 5.10c
Follow a steep slab right of the overhanging face.

7. Work It On Out 5.12d
The hardest of the short routes.

8. Dampened Enthusiasm 5.12a
A 3-bolt boulder problem to hook anchors.

9. Red Badger 5.11d
The boulder problem right of #5.

Upper Cliff

10. Feeding the Beast 5.12b
Four bolts to anchor.

11. Joyride 12d
A good line on the cliff's left side. Seven bolts.

12. Der Letzer Zug 5.12c
Water streak on the upper shield.

13. Der Reeperbahn 5.13b
The quality 8-bolt arete line.

14. Loading Zone 5.10d
Follow the right-facing dihedral

15. Quintet 5.10b/c
This 2 pitch route climbs a right-facing criss-crossing dihedral that encounters five roofs. Belay on a ledge. The 2nd pitch climbs a fist-sized crack over a roof (5.10d).

16. Give the Dog a Bone 5.13a
Climb an arching corner past two bolts. When it bends right, turn the roof and continue to a ledge.

17. Coney Island Baby 5.12 R
Begin as for 12, but stay on the right-facing dihedral to a vertical crack system.

18. Gagger 5.14a
Thin edges up the steep wall below 17's arch. Turn arch to continue up headwall. No American ascents to date. Nine bolts.

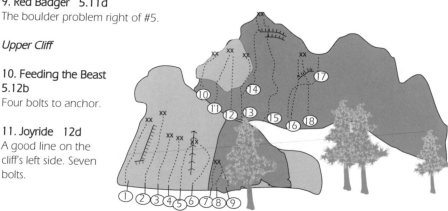

Easter Rock

Easter Rock has rapidly become the sport crag of choice since it was first developed in the mid-90's. Unlike many other Boulder Canyon cliffs, Easter Rock is quite steep—so steep, in fact, that it often stays dry in the rain. Approach from a well-worn trail near the fire hazard sign. The approach consists of steep switchbacks and doesn't follow the obvious gully. Routes are listed from left to right, but keep in mind that many routes are link-ups or share bolts. These are most often prefaced with a letter following the route's number.

1. Warm Up 5.10c
A short route that follows a blunt arete.

2. Barbarians 5.10b or 5.12b
A technical endeavor with a hard to read crux on the upper wall. Nine bolts in all but it is possible to traverse left to the anchors on *Warm Up* for a 10b variation.

3. Empire of the Fenceless 5.12a
The striking sharp arete. Traverse in from the left and follow seven bolts to rope-twisting Metolius anchors.

4. Tell-Tale Heart 5.12b
Guaranteed to elevate your heart rate. Eight bolts lead up discontinuous cracks to an overhanging dihedral, then over a pumpy slope-fest roof.

4a. Nevermore 5.12d
A great link-up that climbs all of *Tell-Tale's* difficulties, then traverses right to a big dyno and to an anchor right of #4's.

Matt Reynolds on *Empire of the Fenceless*

Easter Rock

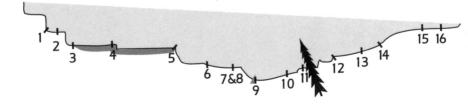

5. Elanor 5.11c
A good warm-up as it's loaded with rests. Follow an right-trending, left-facing, overhanging dihedral system. The anchors are a long stretch for short folks. 8 bolts.

5a. Evermore 5.12c
From the sit-down rest on *Elanor*, move left to a dyno shared by *Nevermore*.

6. Thunderdome 5.12a
An outstanding crack route with a crux above the roof. If you do the trad thing, this is worth ticking. Traverses right or can start up *Dark Night*.

7. The Riddler 5.11c
A tricky route that tackles a slimy slab before joining the dihedral. Climbs like an Eldorado route except for the seven closely-spaced bolts. The anchors are above a ledge and can't be spotted from below.

8. Dark Knight 5.11d
A link-up with its own identity. Begin up *The Riddler* past two bolts, then attack a crux boulder problem undercling at the roof before finishing on the pumpy finale' of *Elanor*.

9. The Joker 5.11b
A six-bolt outing that begins from a tottering block before moving into a funky technical dihedral. Six bolts to anchors by the tree.

10. Catwoman 5.12d
A tricky boulder problem up a seam eventually leads to a funky crux on the short headwall. More continuous than it appears. Five bolts to the anchors near the tree.

11. The Penguin 5.12b
Start just right of the leaning tree and follow 5 bolts up a dihedral, to a sloping ledge, and up the headwall on *Catwoman*.

12. Willard 5.11c
A testpiece of stemming prowess. Six bolts define this polished corner.

13. White Man Can't Jump 5.12a
A somewhat silly outing up a virtual chimney to a sit down rest before a single trick move gains the anchors.

14. Dynamic Duel A0
Aid up manufactured pockets, bolted on holds, and other atrocities to an anchor.

15. The Flying Beast 5.12d
Continuously difficult climbing out a severely overhanging dihedral. A final dyno has earned the nickname "the Bobbit move" for the proximity of a rock spike to one's belay loop.

16. Rain Shadow 5.12b
A tricky but excellent crack route that pulls the roof right of *The Flying Beast*.

17. Wagging the Nub 5.11d

Why does a dog wag his tail? Because he's smarter than the tail. If the tail were smarter, it would wag the dog. Begin to the right of the previous route and climb a mixed gear and bolt pitch past four bolts. A second pitch climbs a crack/flake of various sizes (mostly wide) to a 2-bolt anchor.

Castle Rock

Castle Rock is, without a doubt, at the heart of Boulder Canyon climbing. It was the sight of some of the area's earliest hard routes.

The approach to Castle Rock involves driving 12 miles up the canyon until the Castle becomes apparent on the left at the 29.3 mile marker. Pull off onto the dirt road that circles the rock itself. This convenience means the walking part of the approach involves little more than putting on your sandals and heading to the route of your choice.

Descending from the summit involves scrambling north, then following the path of least resistance down a series of ledges and ramps (4th class). If you find it, there is one possible rappel from a tree with slings. I recommend being very comfortable with downclimbing, as this can turn hairy with the slightest route finding error.

Photo on following page

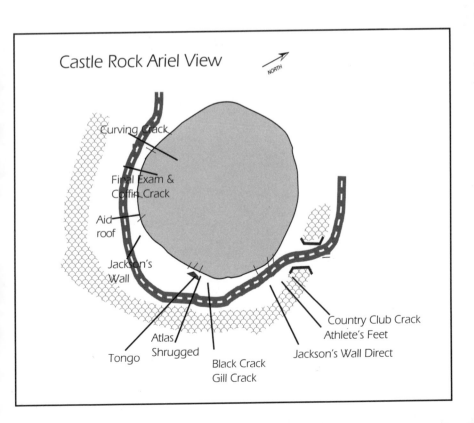

Castle Rock Ariel View

NORTH

Curving Crack

Final Exam & Coffin Crack

Aid roof

Jackson's Wall

Tongo

Atlas Shrugged

Black Crack
Gill Crack

Country Club Crack
Athlete's Feet

Jackson's Wall Direct

A bit of local color surrounds *The Final Exam*. Royal Robbins and Pat Ament made the first ascent of this notably short route while some tourists watched. " That must be the final exam", they commented. In *Rocky Heights*, an early Boulder guidebook, Jim Erickson described *Final Exam* as an "overglorified boulder problem". Ament's response in his guidebook High Over Boulder occurs in the route description: "If one thinks this is an overglorified boulder problem, just try it as such."

Castle Rock

1. Polyester Leisure Suit 5.11a
A bolted route on the left part of the crag. Pulls a roof and heads to a tree anchor. Worthwhile if you're already beneath it.

2. Comeback Crack 5.10b/c
An excellent finger and hand crack with the crux near the ground. Walk off or rap from *Curving Crack's* funky anchors.

3. Curving Crack 5.9+
A popular outing up a left-trending arching dihedral. Polished and Yosemite-like with a crux near the top.

4. Final Exam 5.11a
Another Castle Rock classic, this route is located near the northern terminus of the rock (closest to the road) and is characterized by a finger crack through a roof. (It is just left of *Coffin Crack*). This pitch is extremely good when combined with the *Pass/Fail Option (11a)* above.

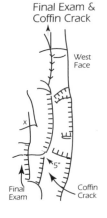

Final Exam & Coffin Crack

West Face

Final Exam

Coffin Crack

5. Coffin Crack 5.10b
A difficult offwidth that passes several roofs on it's way to the summit of Castle Rock.

6. Cussin' Crack 5.7
A good route that can be dispatched in two long pitches or guided in four short ones. Each pitch is harder than it looks. Begin in the large cave/chimney affair and either climb the chimney (5.4) or the slab to the right (5.7R). Proceed to a notch then out a deceptive steep (but short) wall to a large belay ledge. The next pitch will have you cussin' as you ascend the slick dihedral. Belay just beneath the summit and descend the north face.

7. Jackson's Wall 5.6
Jackson's Wall often gets slandered for its lack of clean rock, but the route is quite fun, and is a good moderate way to the summit.

The route begins on the SW face in a chimney next to a huge block. The slab out right is better climbing but is unprotected and more difficult (perhaps 5.7+). Continue up the chimney/trough (5.5) and belay on a good ledge.

Continue up the left-facing dihedral to a roof, step left past a large chockstone (5.6), then back up and right to easy ground. Follow this easier climbing to the top.

Descend via the north face downclimb.

8. Tongo 5.11a R-
A good route that, with the exception of the first moves (11a), proves a safe outing. Climb up (crux) to a right-angling shallow ramp which leads to a bolt anchor. The second pitch is well protected and climbs the dihedral above (11a). These may be led as one long pitch.

9. Atlas Shrugged 5.11d R
A great route but a trying lead, this is most often toproped from the first pitch of *Tongo*. A ground up lead requires some type of extension to place the critical nut (a #1 Rock).

10. Black Crack 5.9+
The ugly fire-scarred route used to set up a toprope on *Gill Crack*.

11. Gill Crack 5.11d/12a
Often toproped, sometimes soloed, rarely led. The short but difficult pin-scarred finger crack.

Castle Rock

12. Jackson's Wall Direct 5.10a
aka South Face

This is a terrific route of an easier grade with excellent belay stances. The route starts with a short right-facing dihedral that begins 30 feet left of *Country Club Crack*. Climb into the shallow dihedral then hand traverse left to a good ledge before the dihedral begins to curve right.

The next pitch traverses left into cracks which lead upwards. A high and low variation exist; both are exciting and involve pro at your feet. Follow these cracks to another crack system up and left. Belay once a good stance is reached.

A fourth class pitch winds up and right to the summit.

Descend via the north face descent.

13. Athlete's Feat 5.11b

Athlete's Feat is a classic both historically and in its climbing. As you sketch up the more difficult pitches, keep in mind that Royal Robbins and Pat Ament did the first free ascent in 1964. Begin at the top of a pointed boulder just to the left of *Country Club Crack* (southeast corner) where the crux of the route is the 5.11 mantle onto a slab. Belay above and left at a bolted stance. The route is hard to miss above this point: Pitch 2 climbs a steep and polished lieback crack (hard 5.10). Pitch 3 climbs another right-facing corner. The fourth pitch is quite a bit harder than it looks—following broken cracks in a gully-like affair. The fifth pitch takes one of two cracks above the belay.

14. Country Club Crack 5.11b/c

Country Club Crack might be considered the *Naked Edge* of Boulder Canyon. This route is particularly enjoyable as it allows you to tick an "11c" crack without having to climb an 5.11c crack (the crack crux is easier 5.11).

Jane Sears on Country Club Crack
Photo by Dan Hare

This SW facing route is located near the bridge, and begins near a large boulder to the right of a prominent spike. The crux is the ten feet of face climbing which gains the 5.8 crack of the first pitch. Belay on a good ledge.

The second pitch is obvious and ascends a scarred hand and finger crack past several suspicious pieces of fixed gear. Two 5.10 roofs are encountered before reaching a tough flared finger section. Many people, myself included, try to weasel a no-hands knee lock rest at the second roof, but I always waste more energy in the attempt to extricate my jammed knee than I regain with the "rest". Anyway, this pitch ends on a ledge with boulders, from where you can rappel with two ropes if you wish. If you want to summit, ascend the obvious chimney, then traverse to the downclimb on the north side.

THE FLATIRONS

Mia Axon on The Big Picture   5.12c
Photo by Stewart Green

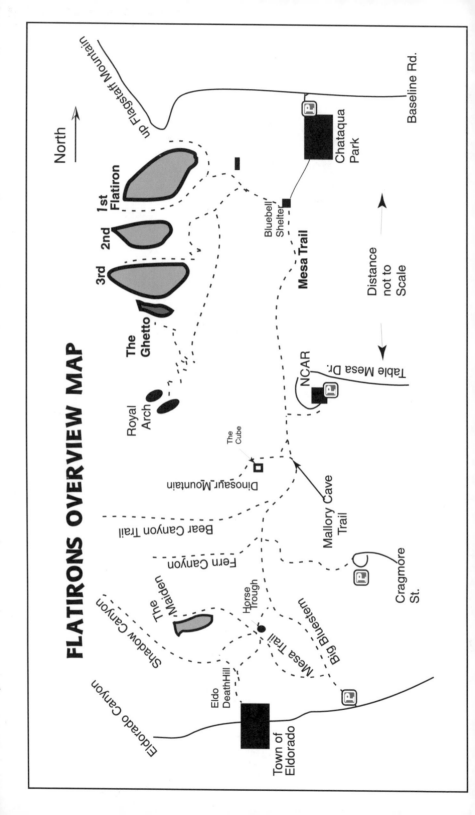

THE FLATIRONS

The Flatirons are hard to miss. They dominate the western skyline of Boulder, and serve as the unofficial symbol of the city. These massive sandstone intrusions are world famous, and provide revenue for the postcard and calendar industry.

Climbing access to the Flatirons is a rather complex issue, both in the approach and the land use arenas.

An excellent trail system runs throughout The Flatirons, and using the Flatiron trail map is the best way to assure yourself of arriving at the base of your chosen climb. We have also included detailed approach info in each description, so you should be able to have a hassle-free climbing day on these fantastic rocks.

As far as land use goes, the Flatirons lie completely under the jurisdiction of Boulder Mountain Parks. One of their jobs is to close various Flatiron formations for raptor nesting. Most years, the closures start in February and continue through July. Obviously this is a huge chunk of the climbing season, and can be discouraging if you've travelled many miles to climb the Third Flatiron and arrive here to discover that it's closed.

At any rate, the traditional areas we'll be dealing with are The Third Flatiron, The First Flatiron, and The Maiden. On these monoliths exist Boulder's longest and oldest routes, as well as what may be the most famous rappel in Colorado. The sport climbs covered on Dinosaur Mountain, Bear and Fern Canyons allow for some wandering in the more remote areas of the park. Check with The Boulder Mountaineer, Neptune Mountaineering or the Boulder Mountain Parks office for accurate info on closures. Of the sport areas, usually only the north side of Fern Canyon experiences closures.

First Flatiron

The First Flatiron is the northernmost of the monoliths and houses some of the longest routes. Hike up from Chautauqua Park and follow the trails labeled to the First Flatiron.

Two options exist for the descent. From the summit locate two eyebolts 100' to the west (two ropes). Rap 25' west to a ledge, scramble 30' to another eyebolt, and rappel a final 60' to the south. The other option involves a scramble down the *South Ridge* along 5.0 terrain. An established trail heads south and drops down between the Second and First Flatirons heading back to the wooden starting platform.

1. North Arete   5.5 R

North Arete is referred to, and deservedly so, as one the best 5.5's in Boulder. It differs from most Flatiron climbs in that it traverses a serrated ridge rather that climbing a broad face. A stunning an obvious line, it follows the broken western skyline of the Flatiron as it rises to the summit. The route has reasonable pro for a Flatiron climb, but does not climb the large face; rather it traverses in from high on the ridge.

Begin by scrambling around the northern side of the First, and hop on the ridge at the point where it leaves the ground. Follow the ridge up as it rises, and head for the summit, passing many false summits and gendarmes. Stay close to the top of the ridge to keep the rating at 5.5 and the protection adequate.

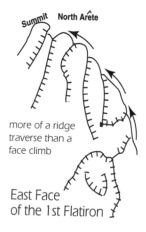

The route can be done in five or six pitches, depending on where you choose to belay.

The Flatirons in morning light.

Sharon Vaughan on
the Direst East Face

3. Baker's Way 5.4

This route crosses the First Flatiron from
the south side, in the gully between the
1st and 2nd Flatirons. Locate the route
by searching for two small pine trees
about 35 feet up from the base. Climb
the slab toward the trees (crux) and
then cruise the right-angling ramps for
a few pitches. Move up and north to
the *North Arete Route*.

4. South Ridge 5.2

This is also the scramble descent route
for the previous climbs. This long 1
pitch route (or 2 shorter ones) begins
between the 1st and 2nd Flatirons in
the little depression. The climbing
generally meanders up ramps, ledges,
and more ramps and ledges. Consider
this more of a hike than a climb.

2. Direct East Face 5.6 R

10 pitches, 1000 feet, a great
route. Stay on the obvious line
as variations will try to lure you
off route. Begin above the
wooden steps and platform at
the base.

1st pitch- 5.6 friction and little
pro. Climb up to a beefy bolt
and continue to a stance.

2nd pitch- Up and left to a
belay ledge at a tree.

3rd pitch- Slabular 5.5 can lead
almost anywhere, but keep a
straight line.

4th and 5th- Straight up on
good holds, a bit steeper.

6th pitch- Up left to a belay
below a wide chimney slot.

7th pitch- Work into the
aforementioned slot to a gully
up to the ridge. Hook up with
North Arete at this point.

A barrage of summiters from an early morning wedding party

Third Flatiron

Approaching the Third is a longish hike, but easy to find. From Chautauqua start up the old road that heads south. Follow this to the Bluebell Shelter. The trail for the Third leaves Bluebell to the west, and winds around through forest and talus for a short while. Follow the trail where it splits from the main trail (signs clearly mark the way) and climbs steeply west again, crossing more talus and snaking through huge boulders. The "East Bench", a tongue/ledge with trees on it, is where you can begin the climbs described below. You can either stash your pack in the rocks near the "Bench" or you can climb with it. I recommend taking at least one pack up with you for water, hiking boots or sandals (as the walk out is hell in rock shoes), and whatever else.

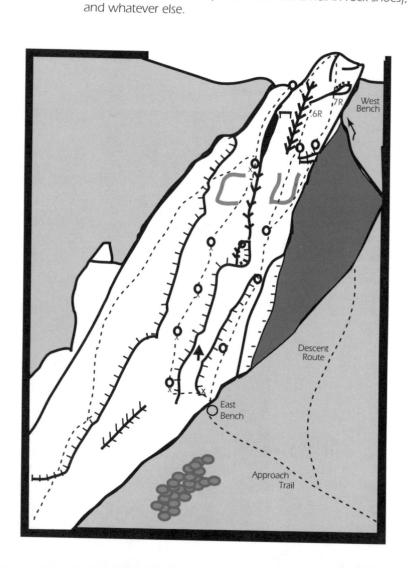

Three rappels from large eyebolts. 1-Rap 45' to the South Bowl, 2- Move south and rappel 50' to Friday's Folly Ledge, 3- Move west on the ledge and rappel 72' to the west to reach the dip below the west face. Caution: on Friday's Folly Ledge if you use the east bolt and rap to the south the rappel is 140'

1. East Face Left   5.5 R

Approach on the Royal Arch Trail from the Bluebell Shelter. Keep an eye out for a rough trail that leads up the canyon to the base of the face (the low side). This 10 pitch route begins at the base of the buttress. The first pitch heads up and right along a rib. Angle to the ramps on the left side of the large overhang for the easier variation, or go straight over it for a 5.7 crack. The following five pitches take you to the top of the Gash and finish on *The Standard Route* described below.

2. The Standard Route   5.4 R

This route on the Third Flatiron definitely rivals *The Bastille Crack* for the most heavily travelled route in Boulder and Colorado. This route has been called the best beginner climb in the world by many people, including Yvon Chouinard. However, the route should not be taken lightly as the pro is scarce and it's very committing. The route is very long, consistently moderate, and exhilarating. The rock is superb. The views are fantastic. What else to you want?

Approach as described on the previous page for routes #2 and 3.

1st pitch- Begin directly below a small tree which sits about 25 feet up the face. Perform a rising traverse to the left (5.0) , passing a huge eyebolt. Drop into the polished trough where it feels comfortable, and aim for another eyebolt on the opposite edge of the trough. Belay at this bolt.

2nd, 3rd, and 4th pitches- Follow similar terrain up, stopping to belay at three identical bolts along the way. The fourth pitch crosses the painted letter "C" from bottom left to upper right and belays at the last of the bolts, right below a huge chimney called "The Gash".

5th pitch- from here head up and left, over a small roof (5.2), then run your rope out to a decent ledge.

6th pitch- Head up a little more until an obvious traverse right can be made on to "Kiddy Car Ledge" which is directly below the summit slab. Either belay or continue up incredible rock (5.4) with little pro to the summit.

Third Flatiron

3. Extra Point

You are in essence a football attempting to climb the six pitches, score the extra point through the giant **U** acting as goal posts, and summit the 3rd. Begin as for *The Standard Route*. After passing the small tree head up staying on the north side of a large gully system. The route encounters a sloping ledge system about three pitches up. Several variations exist through the **U** area and to the summit, either 5.6 R or 5.7 R. The left route includes an extra belay as it merges with the Standard Route before the summit pitch.

Routes 4 and 5 are not shown on the drawing as they are on the west face of the 3rd. If you don't feel like going home after summiting the third, these routes are encountered on a ledge after the third rappel.

4. Friday's Folly 5.8

1, 2, or 3 pitches depending on how you choose to do it. Begin near the southwest corner of the ledge. This steep and exposed route takes you along a crack, then over a roof, and finally to *Friday's Folly* ledge. You can either rap here or head up to the South Bowl, exposed 5.7. From here you can locate the rap anchors on the right side of the ledge or head up the short pitch to the summit, 5.7. Refer to topo for further details.

5. Saturday's Folly 5.8+

This route can be led or toproped if your rope is still in place from the rappel. Start near some chopped bolts and head up to a crack with very obvious piton scars. Head right and ascend the face, turn the roof on the left, and finish at the rap anchor.

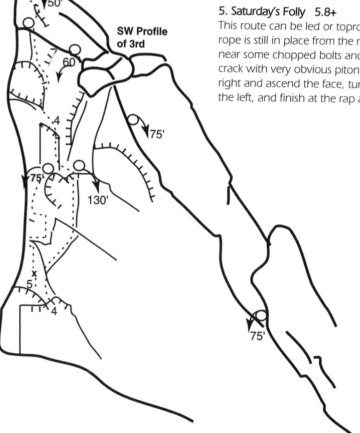

SW Profile
of 3rd

Dinosaur Mountain
Bear Canyon

Dinosaur Mountain and Bear Canyon are popular sport climbing areas due to their tranquil location nestled in the Flatirons. Dinosaur is home of the often photographed *Cornucopia* and *Power Bulge*. Unlike other Flatiron areas, they aren't victims of seasonal closures. The overview map below as well as the more detailed one on the next page will help orient you to these two neighboring areas.

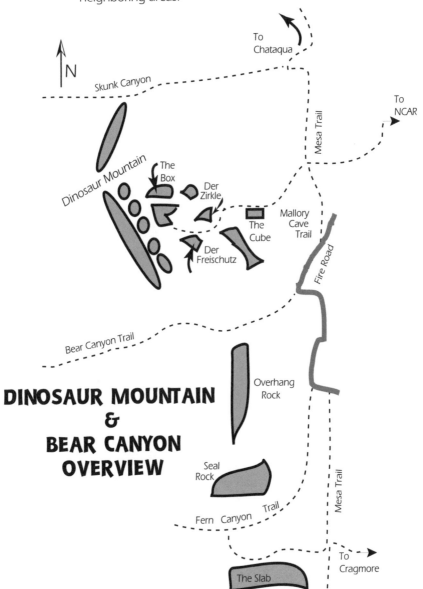

**DINOSAUR MOUNTAIN
&
BEAR CANYON
OVERVIEW**

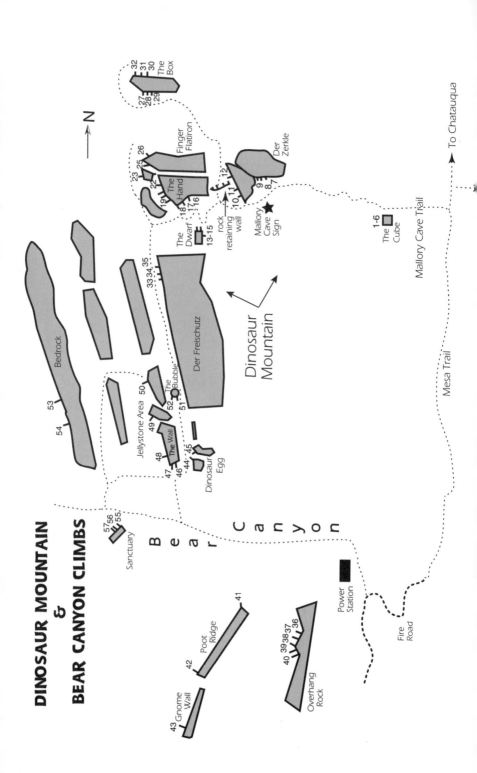

DINOSAUR MOUNTAIN
&
BEAR CANYON CLIMBS

N

The Box

32
31
30
27
28
29

Finger Flatiron

23 25 26
22
19 18 17 16
20
The Hand

12
11
10
9 8 7
Der Zerkle

rock retaining wall

Mallory Cave Sign

1-6
The Cube

The Dwarf
13-15

33 34 35

Der Freischutz

Dinosaur Mountain

Bedrock

53
54

Jellystone Area 50
52 The Bubble
49 51
48
47 46
The Wall
44 45
Dinosaur Egg

57 56
55
Sanctuary

B e a r   C a n y o n

Power Station

41
Poot Ridge

42

40 39 38 37
36
Overhang Rock

43 Gnome Wall

Fire Road

Mesa Trail

Mallory Cave Trail

To Chatauqua

Dinosaur Mountain & Bear Canyon
at a glance

The Cube
1. Flake 5.10
2. Crack 5.11
3. Android Powerpack 5.12d/13a
4. Yellow Christ 5.12b
5. The Tree Swing 5.8
6. Merest Excrescences 5.12b

Der Zerkle
7. Knot Carrot 5.10d/11a
8. Touch Monkey 5.10d/11a
9. April Fools 5.11d
10. Hot If You're Not 5.11d
11. Wing Ding Ding-aling Down She Goes
    5.11b or 5.9+
12. What If You're Not? 5.8

The Dwarf
13. Hiss and Spray 5.12a
14. Eat Cat Too 5.11
15. Cat-O-Nine Tails

The Hand
16. Back in Slacks 5.11b/c
17. Power Bulge 5.12c
18. Meals of Truman 5.11c
19. Father on Fire 5.10+
20. Perfect Kiss 5.11+
21. Cardboard Cowboy 5.11
22. New Saigon 5.11b/c

Shark's Fin
23. Screams Bunny 5.10
24. Archer 5.11a/b

Finger Flatiron
25. Monodoigt 5.11b
26. Nude Figures in a Hollow Fruit 5.11a

The Box
27. Discipline 5.12a
28. Cornucopia 5.13a
29. Unnamed 5.12
30. Spank the Dog
31. The Fact of a Doorframe 5.11b
32. Aunt Jennifer's Tigers 5.10c

Der Freischutz
33. Bidoigt 5.9+
34. Durgs 5.11b/c
35. Sex 5.10c/d

Overhang Rock/The Big Picture
36. Snake Watching 5.13a
37. Tits Out for the Lads 5.12b
38. The Big Picture 5.12c
39. The Missing Link

Poot Ridge
41. Shoot to Thrill 5.12a
42. Stoned Operation 5.11c/d

Gnome Wall
43. Enchanted Forest 5.11b

Dinosaur Egg
44. Coming Attraction 5.10a
45. Sneak Preview 5.11b/c

The Wall
46. Thought Control 5.9+
47. Crack System 5.8+
48. Auspice 5.11c R-

Clay Wall
49. The Sculpture 5.11c
50. The Fiend 5.1c/d

The Bubble
51. Hot Spit
52. Cold Sweat 5.11d

Bedrock
53. Liquid Crystal
54. Megasauras 5.10d

Sanctuary
55. Fire 5.12c
57. Sanctuary 5.12

Dinosaur Mountain

The most common approach to Dinosaur Mountain is via the Mallory Cave Trail. Refer to the Trail Map for greater detail. Start at NCAR, hike towards the Mesa Trail, then follow the signs to Mallory Cave. The trail heads mainly west toward Dinosaur Mountain. The trail crosses the Mesa Trail and continues west. This is a great year-round crag due to its somewhat southern exposure.

Pat Perrin on Hot Spit (5.11c)

The Cube

The first routes encountered on the trail are on The Cube.
Anchors on top allow this unique rock to be toproped

1. Flake   5.10
Perhaps named after the first ascensionist,
this is the leftmost flake as you're facing the
rock.

2. Crack   5.11
No guesses on the origin of that name.

3. Android Powerpack   5.12d/13a
A sequential route first toproped by
Christian Griffith and Harrison Decker,
though it doesn't sport an artsy
"Verve-esque" name as do most of C.G.'s
routes.

4. Yellow Christ   5.12b
Named by Griffith after the famous
Gauguin painting.

5. The Tree Swing   5.8
The easiest way up or down.

6. Merest Excrescences   5.12b
This route lies just to the right of the tree
and is in the center of the west face.

Fred Knapp on *Touch Monkey* 5.10d/11a
Photo by Dan Hare

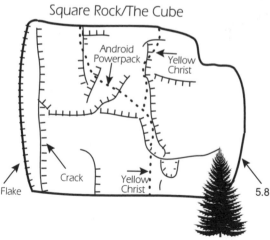

Square Rock/The Cube

Android
Powerpack

Yellow
Christ

Crack

Yellow
Christ

Flake

5.8

Der Zerkle

Follow the trail upward with an eye for small Mallory Cave signs tacked on trees. Der Zerkle is directly across from one of these signs in a little alcove about 1/8 mi. past The Cube. The chalk will give it away.

7. Knot Carrot 5.10d/11a
Goes up a dihedral to a roof. Three bolts up to a two-bolt belay.

8. Touch Monkey 5.10d/11a
Located on the left. Climbs steep huecos to same anchors as for 7. First clip is a bit scary.

9. April Fools 5.11d
On the ramp above the previous routes lies April Fools. This has as much to do with the reported 5.10 rating as it does with the first ascent date.

Hike up meandering steep boulders to reach the next climbs. The routes are located near the rock retaining wall.

10 Hot If You're Not 5.11d
Three bolts above the bouldering wall. At the time of printing one hanger was missing at the anchors. Walk off.

Not shown on the map is a 5.8 trad crack climb, *Final Solution*, between #10 and #11.

11. Wing Ding Ding-a-ling Down She Goes 5.11b or 5.9+
The rating is mostly due to opening moves, as the rest of the climb is significantly easier. Unfortunately, the first bolt is now gone requiring one to boulder out the crux. A toprope can also be set up by doing #10 and scrambling along the top to the anchors. You can also avoid the initial difficulty by hand traversing in from the left.

12. What If You're Not? 5.8
This 4-bolt line has become a popular first sport lead. Great huecoed holds and fun moves. Bring up long slings for toproping. Rap or scramble down.

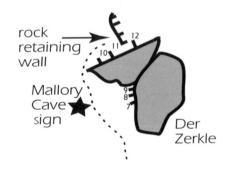

The Dwarf

Instead of following the trail to Mallory Cave, cut left over another small rock wall just before a large boulder that is very overhanging on the trail-side. Scramble up a boulder and follow a hard-to-discern trail until the ravine levels out and The Dwarf, a boulder with several topropes, comes into view.

13. Hiss and Spray 5.12a
Two small roofs face east. Bolts on top for the toprope anchor. A former lead that was chopped.

14. Eat Cat Too 5.11
Right of *Hiss and Spray*.

15. Cat-O-Nine Tails 5.12a
Ascend pebbles to the right of #14

The Hand

Now you are in the heart of Dinosaur Mountain and the home of some of Boulder's best bolted routes. The Hand is just uphill from the Dwarf. This area began seeing development in 1987, largely by Paul Glover and the transplanted Texan porn-star-wannabe Hank Caylor. Does the route name *Power Bulge* stem from these career aspirations? As the idea of rap-bolting was just gaining a foothold at this time, Dinosaur Mountain was littered with controversy. But as The Monkees said, "That was then, this is now."

16. Back in Slacks 5.11b/c
The rightmost route up overhanging huecoed terrain. Bolts and a pin to a double-bolt belay.

17. Power Bulge 5.12c
Interesting climbing and some sequential sections. Follow bolts up the steep huecoed wall which exits on a tricky vertical slab.

18. Meals of Truman 5.11c
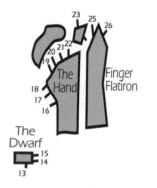
Begin in a dirty hole to a ring bolt, then to a crack system. Pitons protect the crack, but you may wish to back them up.

To reach the next series of routes, follow the Hand as it curves around to the north. Scramble up a gully or climb the rock behind it and drop in from the west. You may wish to anchor the belayer as the gully is loose and solid stances are hard to find.

19. Father on Fire 5.10+
A bolted crack (supplemental gear is nice) on a west-facing overhanging wall. Double bolt anchor.

20. Perfect Kiss 5.11+
Left of #20 is an overhanging thin face route with some friable holds. The second pitch up the very overhanging roof is **Rock Atrocity 13c.**

21. Cardboard Cowboy 5.11b
A pumpy and interesting route that follows bolts right of *New Saigon*. A little runout at the top which makes clipping the anchors feel even more difficult than it is.

22. New Saigon 5.11b/c
Great climbing up huecos. Three bolts to a two-bolt anchor.

Shark's Fin

Hike north up along the same ridge as The Hand until you reach a small pinnacle.

23. Screams Bunny 5.10
Found on the west is a short wall with one bolt.

24. Archer 5.11a/b
On the north face is an obvious block. *Archer* climbs the left crack. Bring a rack with some smaller sizes and wires.

SW on Back in Slacks Dan Hare photo

Finger Flatiron

Found just north of Shark's Fin is a convex wall that offers some slabby footsy climbing.

25. Monodoigt 5.11b
Named for its most significant feature, a one finger pocket.

26. Nude Figures in a Hollow Fruit 5.11a or 5.10b
This north side face route ascends past three bolts to the top of the finger. It is quite easy to avoid the difficulties, creating a 5.10b climb.

Sharon Vaughan on Nude Figures

The Box

Continue upward and to the north/northwest to reach The Box, home of two stellar routes and a couple of other O.K. routes, included because one of the authors is the first ascensionist.

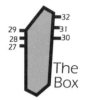

The Box

27. Discipline   5.12a
The geological equivalent of Cindy Crawford—a beautiful face with great curves, and (presumably) hard to tick.

28. Cornucopia   5.13a
This is the beautiful lefthand bolt line. Bring a #3 Friend, no anchor.

29. Unnamed   5.12
A toprope to the left of *Cornucopia* ascends a blunt arete embedded with pebbles.

30. Spank the Dog   5.12b/c
A short but good route on the north side of the Box.

31. The Fact of a Doorframe   5.11b
A balancy route that climbs past bolts and a single pin (which will eventually fall out).

32. Aunt Jennifer's Tigers   5.10c
Follow a crack to some bolts, Bring some RP's and 2-2.5 Friends.

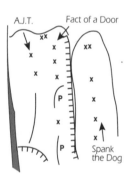

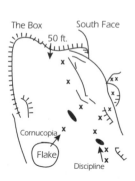

Dale Goddard on the first ascent of *Cornucopia*
Photo by Dan Hare

Der Freischutz

The best way to reach this piece of rock is to start in the gully facing *Back in Slacks*. Looking due south from this gully (towards Bear Canyon) you will make out a funky finger-like summit. The following three routes gain the summit of Der Freishutz.

33. Bidoigt 5.9+
Probably should have been named *Rock & Roll*. Start off of the large boulder below the arete. Climb up a thin face to a TCU placement. Mantle to the small ledge and clip a high bolt (scary if you're short). Climb into a crack then onward to the top. Bring up 1/2 & 3/4 TCU, a #11/2 Friend or some equivalent stopper and a long sling.

34. Drugs 5.11b/c
Just to the right of *Bidoigt* lies this brilliantly pumpy yet technical pebble climb. Start beneath the undercut roof and move onto the vertical wall. Bring long runners for the anchors or belay your second from above, as the anchors are set back from the edge.

35. Sex 5.10c/d
A short climb just right of drugs that angles right a bit.

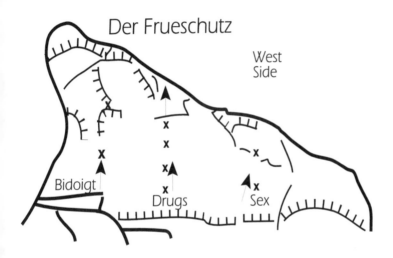

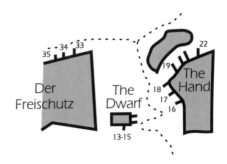

Bear Canyon

Bear Canyon is reached by hiking up from the Mesa Trail.
Parking at NCAR and taking the Mesa Trail south is probably
your best bet if you're unfamiliar with town. (It is also possible to
park on Bear Mountain Drive off Lehigh, but the trailhead is
poorly labeled). The Mesa Trail eventually becomes a fire road.
Cross Bear Creek at a culvert and continue up a large
switchback veering north to a power station. A sign for Bear
Canyon points west as you reach the top of a big bend. The
Bear Canyon trail soon heads west past the power station. Not
far after this a long thin ridge, Overhang Rock, appears to the
south. *Thought Control* can be seen below the trail, rising from
the creek.

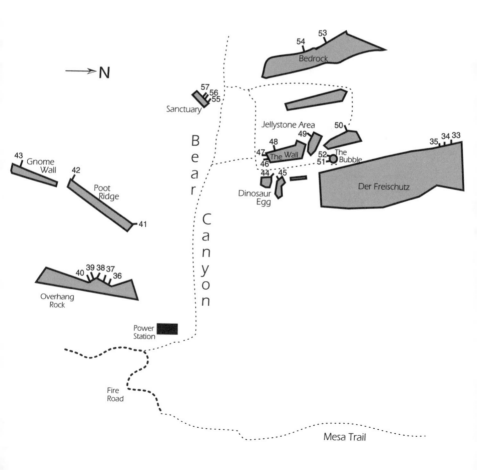

Overhang Rock

Overhang Rock is a beautiful multicolored lichened wall that resembles a giant movie screen.

36. Snake Watching 5.13a
A very long (130') route with the crux at the first bolt and another between the two sets of anchors. Two ropes get you off, especially if you're into bondage. Seriously, the rap can be a bit tricky.

37. Tits Out for the Lads 5.12b
Found right of #36. One tough move can be a stopper on this climb. Rap off.

38. The Big Picture 5.12c
Located in the center of the west face lies this technically sustained route.

39. The Missing Link 5.12b
A good route with distinct cruxes, especially at the upper roof.

40. Unnamed 5.11d
The only "warm-up" on the rock. Tricky.

The Big Picture/Overhang Rock

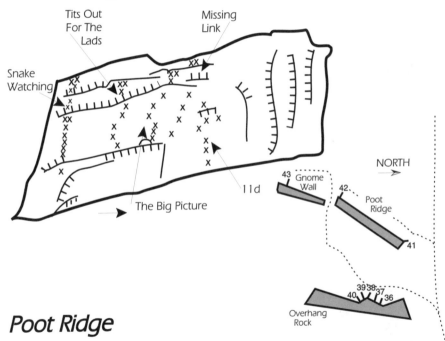

Poot Ridge

Located above Overhang Rock. Only two climbs, but *Shoot to Thrill* is very good and worth doing as you pass by.

41. Shoot to Thrill 5.12a
Climbs up the aesthetic yellow prow. Devious moves provide most of the difficulty on this surprisingly pumpy route.

42. Stoned Operation 5.11c/d
Follow the broken ridge southwest to the first good-looking clean face. The route begins by pulling a roof, but the crux is a bit higher.

Gnome Wall

 The best approach is from the west side of Overhang Rock. Hike up and go through the first gap in Poot Ridge.

43. Enchanted Forest   5.11b
Six bolts just left of an arete on the west face.

Dinosaur Egg

 Continue up the main Bear Canyon trail west. A trail will break off north and lead to several formations. Dinosaur Egg is to the east and really is comprised of more than one boulder. This is the first climbable feature of the north side of Bear Canyon.

44. Coming Attraction   5.10a
Sharp four-bolt arete with no anchor. Scramble down. The infamous Pete Zoller's first new route.

45. Sneak Preview   5.11b/c
A good route on slopey pockets and sharp edges. The preferred warm-up for the really gnarly routes.

Bruce Miller on Sneak Preview 5.11b/c

Jellystone Area

This major ridge is just above the Dinosaur Egg area and is divided into three sections of rock

The Wall

The large wall that comprises the ridge proper is home to some excellent routes.

Anonymous climber on Thought Control 5.9

46. Thought Control 5.9+
Start out of/near the creek and go up the bolted arete. Pull a slanting roof, move right and finish at a two-bolt anchor. Rap to the west. A little spooky for a sport route.

47. Crack System 5.8+
Again begin out the creek, the crack angles left. Although you pass two bolts, bring a rack as well. Not popular.

48. Auspice 5.11c R-
Move around to the west of the wall and locate a route with painted hangers. Go up a slanting crack and then up the face. The upper wall is unprotected but easier than the lower bit. Same anchors as #46, and rap to the west.

Clay Wall

Comprised of the middle rocks of Jellystone Area

49. The Sculpture 5.11c
Ascend the left side of this southwest facing toprope.

50. The Fiend 5.13c/d
Brilliant overhanging stemming dihedral that has only seen two ascents at the time of this printing. Gear, bolts, and pins protect this climb with some blind moves.

Author's side story on the Fiend:

A word of caution. In the Fall of 1993, local hardman and all-around nice guy Mike Downing dislocated his knee cap on the crux back-step-Egyptian-knee-drop-auto-fellatio move. His partners evacuated him to where the ambulance dudes and dudettes could get him morphine.

For the remainder of the day, Mike didn't even know what year it was and probably forgot the bear sighting earlier that morning. The moral of the story is watch out for weird moves and bears and bring your own drugs so you won't have to wait for the rescue crew.

The Bubble

Several routes can be enjoyed on this large boulder found between the Jellystone Area and the next ridge to the east. These overhanging routes lie on the south side.

51. Hot Spit 5.11c
An overhanging huecoed wall to a two-bolt anchor. If this went on any longer it could be the best route in Bear Canyon.

52. Cold Sweat 5.11d
The bolted layback left of *Hot Spit*. A worthy dynamic route.

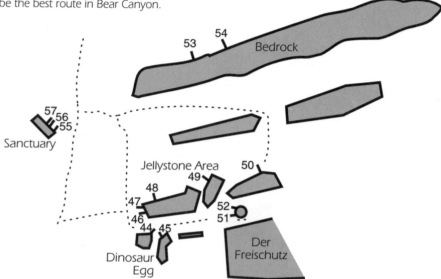

Bedrock

This is the last northern ridge covered in the Bear Canyon/ Dinosaur Mountain Area. Follow the trail to the westernmost ridge on the north side.

53. Liquid Crystal 5.11c
This is the first route you come to as you break north from the main trail (about 600 ft.) Smooth, featureless, bolted face.

54. Megasauras 5.10d
Located to the left of *Liquid Crystal*. Bolted, but gear is needed for an anchor (1.5"-2" cams are recommended).

Sanctuary

Head to the main Bear Creek trail and climb west. On the south side of the trail will appear the next crag on our tour, Sanctuary. It is a toprope wall on the south side.

55. Fire 5.12c
Fantastic route ascending a pockey pebbley arete.

57. Sanctuary 5.12
The furthest right of the three climbs ascends a black water streak.

56. Love 5.12d
Fun on pebbles and pockets.

Fern Canyon

The routes in Fern Canyon can only be described as quality. The hike passes quickly as the scenery captures all of your attention. Unfortunately the season is limited to August through January due to the nesting raptors.

If you hike from the cul-de-sac at the end of Cragmoor, using the South Fork of the Shannahan, stay on this trail after you cross the Mesa Trail. If you come from NCAR just keep an eye out for the Fern Canyon signs. Remain heading west and eventually the trail will abut The Slab, a large formation in Fern. Cross a small creek and meander up switchbacks. Most all of the crags are accessed via social trails.

The information for the Fern section of this book is credited to the late Bill DeMallie who compiled a handout in the late 80's.

Jack Roberts on Undertow 5.12b
Photo by Rod Walker

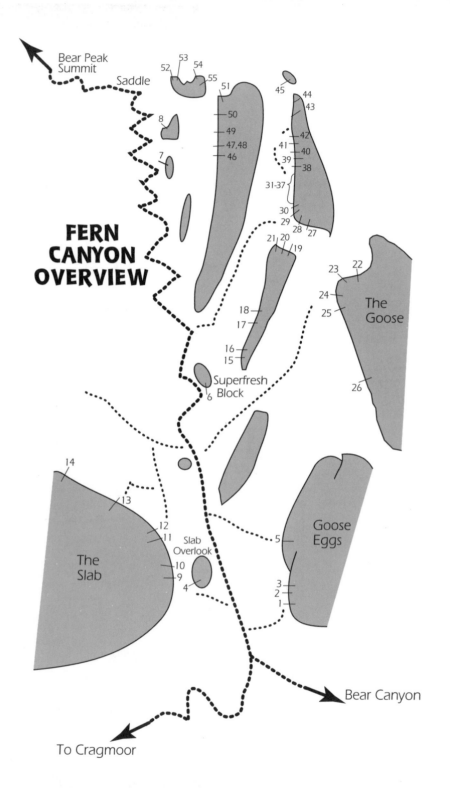

FERN CANYON OVERVIEW

Bear Peak Summit

Saddle

The Goose

The Slab

Slab Overlook

Superfresh Block

Goose Eggs

Bear Canyon

To Cragmoor

Fern Canyon
at a glance

Trail Routes
1. Sea and the Mirror   5.10c
2. Fruity Pebbles   5.9-
3. Power Bacon   5.10-
4. Out of Africa   5.13a
5. Rude Welcome   5.11c
6. Superfresh   5.12c/d
7. Mentor   5.12b
8. A Quickie   5.11a

The Slab
9. Just Another Boy's Climb   5.11d/12a
10. Nasty Boys   unfinished
11. Boys With Power Toys   5.12b
12. Unfinished
13. The Whipping Post   5.11d
14. Undertow   5.12b

The Chains Wall
15. Fertile Crescent   5.11a
16. Castles Made of Sand   5.11c/d
17. Stemmadilemma   5.11d
18. Chains of Love   5.12b/c

The Joint Face
19. Left Joint 10a
20. Rip This Joint   5.10b
21. Right Joint 5.9-

The Goose
22. Pretty Lady 5th
23. Love's Labor Lost 5th
24. Raging Bull   5.12b
25. Wild Horses   5.13a(?)
26. Batman   5.10a(?)

The Gap
27. Exile   5.12a
28. Fluorescent Gray   5.11b/c
29. Everpresent Lane   5.10d
30. Toprope Arete   5.10c

The Ilga Slab
31. Edgemaster   5.10d or 5.10b
32. Slabmaster 5.11d
33. Ilga Grimpeur   5.11b
34. Between Dick and Ilga   5.12a TR
35. A Blessing in Dick's Eyes   5.10c X
36. Bulgemaster   5.11d TR
37. Sporofight   5.11b

The Aretes
38. Superguide   5.9-
39. Iron Cross   5.11a
40. Lightning Bolt Arete   5.11a
41. Haywire   5.9
42. Fountain of Youth   5.10a
43. Unity   5.8
44. Babyback   5.5
45. Kent's Crack   5.12a TR

Neble Horn
46. Rads for Rookies   5.8
47. False Gods, Real Men   5.10a
48. On the Contrary   5.11d TR
49. Violator   5.13c
50. Ruby Slipper   5.11a/b
51. Rainbow Bridge   5.9-

The Mars Block
52. Plain or Peanut   5.11a
53. Devil Dogs   5.13 TR
54. The School   5.12c (?)
55. Creampuff   5.12c/d

Trail Routes

These routes have been grouped together due to their proximity to the main trail. Climbs 1-3 and 5 are on the same wall. Route 4 is beneath a rock peninsula. Routes 6-8 are on trail boulders.

Goose Eggs

Some good warm-ups can be found here as there are several routes of lower grades. Move uphill and north from The Slab Overlook to this hidden wall. Routes 1-3 and 5 can be found here.

1. Sea and the Mirror 5.10c
The righthand warm-up climb on the Breakfast Wall. Climb the huecoed bulge followed by steep face climbing. Four bolts to two bolt anchor.

2. Fruity Pebbles 5.9-
Found in the middle of the Breakfast Wall, this bolted route has a high first bolt that can be supplemented with a Friend and some slings. Traverse left to the anchors.

3. Power Bacon 5.10-
The lefthand line on the Breakfast Wall. Shares anchors with *Fruity Pebbles*.

4. Out of Africa 5.13a

This short overhanging arete hidden under the Slab Overlook is no longer bolted.

5. Rude Welcome 5.11c
Just after passing the Slab Overlook and 20 yards north of the trail is a short overhanging wall, the SE terminus of the Goose Eggs. Welcome to Fern Canyon.

6. Superfresh 5.12c
Obvious overhanging arete on the trail. A superb power route on positive holds.

7. Mentor 5.12b
The tempting huecoed block just off the trail 100 yards below the saddle. The little people will find the reach at bolt #4 tough while the rest of us fall at the final dyno. Excellent steep pitch.

8. A Quickie 5.11a
Hidden uphill from *Mentor* is a short slabular black face.

Dave Crawford on Superfresh 5.12c/d
Photo by Will Niccols

The Slab

Hiroko Ito on the crux of *Just Another Boy's Climb 5.11d/12a*

The Slab

Approach by hiking 100 yards past The Slab Overlook, then cut back left on an obvious trail by a large boulder. Take the first left on a faint trail, then hop across a narrow talus field and pick up the final faint trail. Excellent collection of overhanging endurance climbs.

9. Just Another Boy's Climb 5.11d/12a
Climb a 5.8 slab on the north face of the crag to a nice belay stance, then power up the vertical water streak to an exciting hand traverse right under the roof. Clear the roof by heel hooking left at the last peg. A 1.5 & 2 Friend are handy on the upper crack.

10. Nasty Boys
Unfinished variation on the *Boy's Climb*, moving right from the third bolt.

11. Boys With Power Toys 5.12b
50 ft. right of *Boy's Climb*, vertical wall to a troublesome overlap, then technical face climbing up the right wall of an open corner.

12. Unfinished
An anchor right of 11.

13. The Whipping Post 5.11d
This breaks through the uphill (south) end of the low roof band on the west face of The Slab. Starting in a left-facing corner, hand traverse left out the roof to a thin power crux past the ring bolt. A good shakeout ledge is followed by continuous face climbing on superb black rock.

14. Undertow 5.12b
50 yards uphill from 13, past an arch formation, scramble 20 ft. up to a ledge. An ancient aid route has been transformed into one of Boulder's best beyond vertical jug-hauls. The optional 2.5/3 Friend is placed in a shallow pocket on the right after bolt #5 and reduces a runout, but most people find it unnecessary.

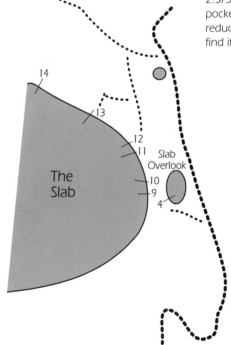

The Chains Wall

Approach by cutting right just after *Superfresh*. Move onto the talus as soon as possible to minimize erosion in the duff on the south side of the gap.

15. Fertile Crescent 5.11a
The first left-facing corner on ridge four. Small wires, and 3 Friend needed.

16. Castles Made of Sand 5.11c/d
Bolted exquisite black face/arete just left of *Fertile*.

17. Stemadilemma 5.11d
Desperate stemming corner uphill from *Castles*. Gear needed includes: wires, TCU's, #2 Friend.

18. Chains of Love 5.12b/c
A nice 5.10 crack pitch (bring a 1.5 & 2 Friend or medium nuts) takes you to the bondage ledge where you can tie yourself to some chains and then whip your partner to a frenzy on the roof.

The Joint Face

The beautiful west-facing high-angle slab uphill from *Chains*: a good morning spot in the summer as it stays in shade till about 4 P.M.

19. Left Joint 5.10a
The left and most direct line on the Joint face. A well traveled, good route for the grade. Some funky gear placements.

20. Rip This Joint 5.10b
The middle route, can be done several ways. Most people clip the lone bolt, then work slightly right then back left to the crack which diagonals left, then to the last bolt on *Left Joint*. This may seem a bit harder than the grade if you climb straight up from the first bolt. Either way, be prepared to work a bit to get in reasonable gear.

21. Right Joint 5.9-
Clip the lone bolt, then move out right to the arete.

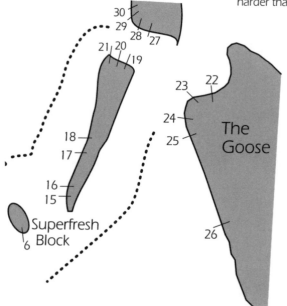

The Goose

Approach by bushwacking NW up the draw past *Rude Welcome*, or dropping through the gap north of the Joint Face. The first two routes are rated fifth class because of the wide reactions (5.5-5.10) to moderate slab climbing.

22. Pretty Lady   5th class
The lefthand line of bolts on the beautiful black slab that forms the west face of the main bulk of the Goose. Friends in sizes 2.5, 3.5, and 4 are needed at the anchor .

23. Love's Labor Lost   5th class
The right-hand line on the Goose. This was missing hangers for awhile, better bring some wires just in case. Friends in 2.5 and 3.5 are need as well.

24. Raging Bull   5.12c
Goes two pitches up the steep orange face around the corner from *LLL*. The first pitch is 5.11a/b and can be done alone if you're not up for the difficulties above.

25. Wild Horses   5.13a?
A long 145' pitch up cracks and open corners to the right of *Raging Bull*, culmination in a steep black water streak (crux). This climbs some attractive rock in a spectacular position, but no second ascent and grade confirmation yet. (Gear: Rocks #7, 7.8, Friends #1.5 and draws)

26. Batman   5.10 R
This involves some fixed gear downhill from *Horses*. Quality unknown.

The Gap

Just north of the Joint Face is a spectacular gap in the ridge which provides nice views of Boulder and also serves as a home for one of the best pitches in the Flatirons, *Exile*.

27. Exile   5.12a
This starts from a precarious belay shelf right in the gap. Follow a beautiful sustained vertical wall to an almost no-hands under the roof, then power left out the roof. If you place natural gear under the roof, use long slings to reduce rope drag over the lip. Gear to bring along includes #.5 and #1 Friends for under the roof.

28. Fluorescent Gray   5.11b/c
Strenuous vertical crack, then out left to continuous technical face climbing on the stepped arete. Double ropes, or pull a single through the nuts when you hit the first bolt. A challenging lead with three 5.11 cruxes, superb positions. Named for the bright lichen by color-blind Bret Ruckman.

29. Everpresent Lane   5.10d
Right-facing corner in brown rock uphill from *Fluorescent Gray*.

30. Toprope Arete   5.10c
The arete left of 29 can be easily toproped off the tree.

Jim Garber on Exile 5.12a
Photo by Will Niccols

The Ilga Slab

100 Yards uphill from the Joint Face is a beautiful wall that harbors some of the best slab pitches in the Flatirons. With the exception of the initial corner on *Sporofight*, the rock quality is outstanding. Access these routes by scrambling up to a ledge with a large spruce.

31. Edgemaster 5.10d or 5.10b
The right-hand line. Climb an easy corner up right, then stretch back left to the first bolt. Continuous 5.9 and 5.10 edging and balance lead to a delicate no hands crux traverse left. One can avoid the crux by topping out before the traverse and scrambling up the ridge to the anchors—this reduces the difficulty to 5.10b. Bring some long slings for bolts 5 & 6.

32. Slabmaster 5.11d
A 5.10 move right off the ledge leads to a sloping shelf, your last rest for the next 40 feet. Follow the line of bolts which sweep in an "S" curve over the bulge. Continuous edging and smearing on immaculate rock.

33. Ilga Grimpeur 5.11b
Starting by the big spruce left of *Slabmaster*, make a few moves up and right to the first bolt (black hanger), then a long traverse left (easier as a foot traverse than as a hand traverse). Follow the water streak up left with increasing difficulty to an extended crux sequence through bolts #4 and #5 and a bit of a runout to an awkward undercling. Step back left and figure out the final tricky 5.10 headwall. The moves are no harder than 11b, but clipping bolt #5 is close to 11c. Most people solve this problem by hanging on the quick. Perfect moves, perfect rock.

34. Between Dick and Ilga 5.12a Toprope
For those with some tips left after the previous three lines, there's an interesting problem between *Dick* and *Ilga*. Instead of scrambling up to the big spruce, start from the ground slightly right of *Dick's Eyes* and diagonal up right to the horizontal break, then over the bulging wall at some huecos. Step back left and take a fall line up to the middle of *Ilga's* crux traverse after bolt #5. Finish on *Ilga*.

35. A Blessing in Dick's Eyes 5.10c X

This follows incipient right-facing corners on the left side of the Ilga slab. Good TR after *Ilga*. Bring some wires and trick gear for cracks. Named for dyed-in-the-wool traditionalist, Dick DuMais, who would appreciate this bold ground-up lead.

36. Bulgemaster 5.11c Toprope
This bisects the narrow face between *Dick* and *Sporofight*, offering better rock and a more direct line than the latter. Turn the overlap three feet left of *Dick*, then continue straight up the face to a difficult sequence up a thin left-angling corner which joins *Sporofight* at the peg.

37. Sporofight 5.11b

The large right-facing corner. Awkward. Bring a light rack to 2".

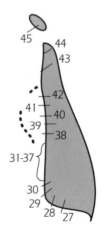

The Aretes

About 50 yards uphill from the Ilga Slab, the smooth wall breaks up into a series of large corners and aretes. Although these routes require the longest approach in Fern, the combination of high quality moderate routes and fantastic views from the summit towers has made this area popular.

38. Superguide 5.9-
The first prominent arete to the right of a left-facing corner. Easy short left-facing corner, strenuous roof-pull off a pedestal, then right to the arete, passing a peg, bolt, and some interesting pockets. A fun moderate route that requites some large wires and Friends in addition to a couple quick draws.

39. Iron Cross 5.11a
This routes contains some height-dependent moves. Move up short corners left of *Superguide* to a stance with two rings. Traverse left along the lip of the roof, then back up right to a large horizontal crack and the final sustained headwall. Make two 50' raps to get off.

40. Lightning Bolt Arete 5.12a
Climb a short, tricky left-facing corner that protects with a #2 Friend, peg and a wire. Then traverse left, catch the bolt to protect the second, and belay at two rings down left in an obnoxious juniper. Follow the arete to a small roof keeping an eye out for a #3 Friend placement after bolt #3. Undercling right to an exciting crux on the arete. Two 50' raps to the south over *Iron Cross* will get you down.

41. Haywire 5.9
Ascend the initial left-facing corner of *Fountain of Youth*, then right to another corner leading to a square cut roof. Finish in a beautiful RP protected corner. Friends up to #2 and wires are needed.

42. Fountain of Youth 5.10a
Another height-related climb. Ascend the easy left-facing corners to a beautiful sharp arete on the right (TCU's are needed just before the first bolt).

The following two lines are approached by scrambling out ledges leading from the small saddle uphill from *Fountain*. Bring up small friends in addition to QD's and wires. There is also a lot of interesting bouldering/toproping on the large blocks here.

43. Unity 5.8+
Gear to 1" will help protect this short tips corner.

44. Babyback 5.5
Perfect short layback corner left of *Unity*. Gear to 3" is needed.

45. Kent's Crack 5.12a TR
This looks like a rubble pile but offers a wild TR on good rock. Begin up a short corner being careful not to knock loose blocks at the base. Cross the overhanging wall via a crack, then dyno up the overhanging arete, finishing on the point. Use two full length slings for the TR anchor.

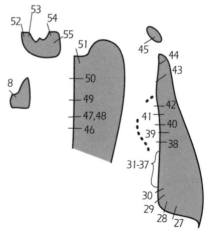

Nebel Horn

These climbs are found on the long ridge extending downhill from Nebel Horn. Approach from the saddle or via a faint trail that cuts NW about 25 yards before *Mentor*. There are also a few crack climbs in this area which see infrequent traffic.

46. Rads for Rookies 5.8
The righthand wall of the *False Gods* alcove, this has surprised more than a few individuals who turned their brains off in anticipation of a jug ladder.

47. False Gods, Real Men 5.10a
The lefthand line in a prominent alcove with a short scramble to the base. The location isn't that great and the rock is grainy in a few spots, but expect fun moves on a slightly overhanging, pumpy wall.

48. On the Contrary 5.11d TR
A deceptively difficult toprope up the angling groove just left of *Real Men*.

49. Violator 5.13c
Halfway between *Real Men* and *Ruby Slipper* is an obvious overhanging arete. Perhaps the cleanest and most compelling 5.13 line in the area, the arete counterpart of *Sphinx Crack*. Note: 13 QD's are needed.

50. Ruby Slipper 5.11a/b
A stunning thin crack in a beautiful multicolored slab. Don't be fooled by the crack—unless you have RP size fingers, this is a delicate face climb. Handle the fragile flakes out left at 1/3 height gently. Rubble alert when topping out. Gear to 1.5" and heavy on the brass.

51. Rainbow Bridge 5.9-
West-facing arete directly under Nebel Horn. Aesthetic positions, great views. Crank the initial overlap (easier swinging south onto jugs), then wander up the moderate arete.

Brad Burrough, Cream Puff

Photo by Will Niccolls

The Mars Block

Fifty yards north of the saddle on the Fern Canyon Trail is a system of huge blocks that harbor some easy scrambling as well as a few problems of greater difficulty.

52. Plain or Peanut 5.11a
Just left of cracks on beautiful concave slab that sweeps up to vertical. The difficulty will vary a bit depending on how far right one moves.

53. Devil Dogs 5.13 TR
The original problem on the Mars block, bark your way up the depressingly smooth slab left of *Plain or Peanut*.

54. The School (of Primitive Behavior) 5.12c
The overhanging west face of the Mars Block, thirty feet left of *Devil Dogs*.

55. Creampuff 5.12c/d

A tasty morsel on the NW corner of the Mars block. Well worth the walk, with good shade until mid-afternoon.

The Maiden

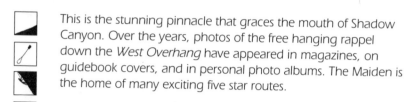

This is the stunning pinnacle that graces the mouth of Shadow Canyon. Over the years, photos of the free hanging rappel down the *West Overhang* have appeared in magazines, on guidebook covers, and in personal photo albums. The Maiden is the home of many exciting five star routes.

The quickest approach to The Maiden begins at the Mesa Trail in Eldorado Canyon. The most difficult part of the approach is locating this trailhead, as the Boulder Mountain Parks have redirected most traffic to the new snazzy South Mesa Trailhead. Anyway...the trailhead is located behind the Eldorado Springs pool on a road that parallels the main Eldo road and is marked by a white sign with faded red lettering.

Follow this trail up a steep hill (this hill was dubbed the "Eldo Death Hill" in the old Basic Boulder Mountain Marathon—but it was encountered at about mile 18). Scoot along the Mesa Trail, past The Matron, and stop at a water trough. Go up the trail until you reach a "path" through the talus. This leads to The Maiden.

To descend from any of the Maiden routes, rappel 120 feet using two ropes to the "Crow's Nest", a precarious stance when viewed from above. This is the very exciting free rappel. Another rappel to the south puts you back on terra firma.

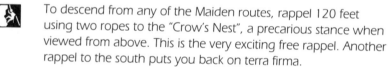

The Maiden

around back

rappel

roof

scary optional belay

West Overhang

East Ridge

Standard Route

cunning Stunt

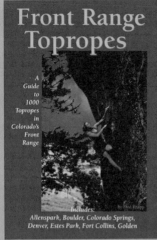

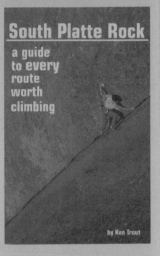
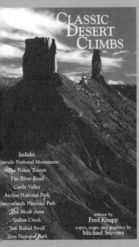

The Maiden

Tim Cumbo on the famous *Maiden* rappel
Photos by Scott Sutton

The Maiden

1. The Standard Route 5.6 R

This is probably the most ascended route on the rock. Start on the westernmost end of the pedestal which houses The Maiden. Climb up a short headwall and belay.

The rock strata, at this point, angles down and left (east). Follow this, then crank up a 5.6 corner and aim left to belay at a tree (this is a bit dangerous for both leader and second, as the traverse is difficult to protect).

More downward traversing takes one to a right-facing dihedral, which spits one out at a cubby hole belay. Climb up an easy slot, then follow the *East Ridge* to the spectacular summit.

2. The East Ridge 5.10c R

This route follows the prominent ridge that is viewed from Boulder. Begin at a handcrack at the bottom of the ridge; the last time I checked, the sling hanging from the crack was merely knotted webbing, so don't whip onto it. Continue up 5.7 terrain to a belay at the base of a short headwall. An alternative 5.7 start begins around the corner on the north face.

Go up the bolt ladder and traverse left to a jug where one can place protection or be nicer to the second by running it out. (You might as well run it out or back clean the gear, as you've already done some scary climbing by trusting those 1/4" bolts).

Next, climb a beautiful pitch along the south side, passing an occasional fixed pin. If you make it all the way to an alcove, communication can be a problem, but the option of belaying at a small notch isn't much better.

Now, swing around to the north side and book it to the summit.

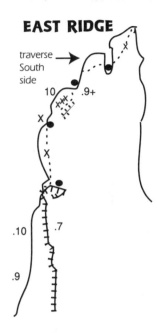

EAST RIDGE

traverse →
South
side

10   .9+

.10   .7

.9

3. The West Overhang 5.11b

This is my personal favorite on The Maiden. Climb to the Crow's Nest via the *Standard Route* or by climbing *Cunning Stunt* — the wide-ish layback almost directly below the Crow's Nest on the north side of The Maiden. (I always like approaching a Maiden's giant overhangs via her cunning stunt, or something like that—although the last bit must be done without protection, which in today's day and age may not be the best idea).

From the Crow's Nest head up the arete on the left past an old bolt, dink in some RP's (long slings on all this stuff is helpful); then go past another old bolt (missing a hanger) and into a slot (crux). Funky moves through the roof/slot put you on the summit.

Now you get to watch your partner squirm. Remember, the less gear you place, the more your partner squirms. Unfortunately, I've never been able to see my partners in anything but a relaxed state.

Variation 5.12b

A harder variation climbs straight up the wall below the slot. Some old fixed gear.

ELDORADO CANYON

Beth Childress on *The West Arete of the Bastille* (5.8+)
Photo by Rod Walker

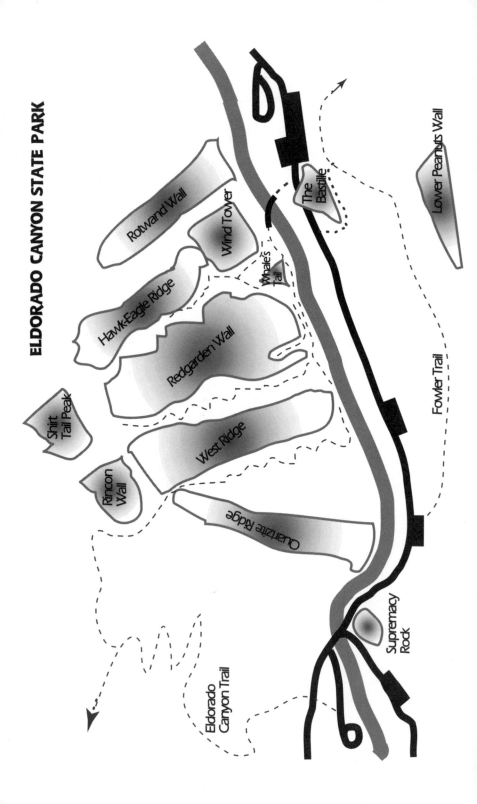

ELDORADO CANYON STATE PARK

Rotwand Wall

Wind Tower

Whale's Tail

The Bastille

Lower Peanuts Wall

Hawk-Eagle Ridge

Redgarden Wall

Shirt Tail Peak

West Ridge

Rincon Wall

Quartzite Ridge

Fowler Trail

Eldorado Canyon Trail

Supremacy Rock

Redgarden Wall
Towers 1 and 2,
The Upper Meadow,
and the Lower Ramp

Tower 1   Tower 2

The
Upper
Meadow

Lower Ramp

Familiarize yourself with this photo as well as the one on the following page as the walls in Eldorado are a bit confusing.

Tower 1

saddle
between
Towers 1 & 2

Redgarden
Wall

Middle
Buttress

Hot Spur

West Ridge

Photo taken from the Fowler Trail

ELDORADO CANYON

Eldorado Canyon has long been the crown jewel of the Boulder region. Before the advent of sport climbing, Eldo was **THE** Rocky Mountain destination area. With a long controversial climbing history, Eldorado was often at the cutting edge of difficulty. Layton Kor pioneered both cutting edge aid routes and bold free lines. His 1958 creation, *The Bulge (5.7)*, still frightens modern leaders (even though Kor rappel-placed a bolt after his first ascent). With Bob Culp, he aided the Naked Edge, the test-piece aid route of the 1960's. Pat Ament, a Kor protegee, was a leading force in new route development as well. During the 1960's he pushed free climbing standards by applying his gymnastic talents to the vertical world. His 1965 ascent of *Supremacy Crack* is regarded as the first 5.11 in America. Jim Ericson followed, ushering in a new standard of technical purity, eschewing pitons and chalk, in favor of a puritanical style. The Ericson camp would come to include Duncan Fergusen who accompanied Ericson on the first free ascent of the *Naked Edge*. Other great influences on Eldorado were Steve Wunsch whose free ascents included the very scary *Jules Verne* and the difficult *Psycho Roof*. In the 1980's Christian Griffith added many difficult lines including *Desdishado* (13c), one of the hardest routes in America at the time.

Wind Tower

The pyramid shaped Wind Tower is the first major feature on the north side of the canyon, just across from the lower parking lot. Approach by crossing South Boulder Creek using the bridge. Turn east, and from here the trail branches north to access the west side routes. A streamside trail running east brings you to the southside routes. The western routes are popular multi-pitch slabular lines with good protection. Beware of loose rock especially on the descent. The southern routes, on the other hand, are steeper and harder to protect.

1. Diffraction 5.10a

Begin up the route just to the right of the *Rainbow Wall* passing mucho antiquated fixed paraphernalia including a Rurp, a bashie, and old bolt, and other unidentifiable material. If you are nervous on this pitch, have your partner lead the ensuing *Metamorphosis*.

2. Metamorphosis 5.9+ R

This is one of my favorite 5.9's in the entire universe, rivaled only by *Plutenka* (5.9-) on Jupiter. Access this by climbing *Diffraction* or, use the route to the right of *Diffraction*, a traversing route aptly named *Yellow Traverse* (5.9 R/X).

Metamorphosis is spectacular. The climbing is always steep and thought provoking; the gear is adequate but not abundant. Climb the left-facing dihedral, or just right of the dihedral, wander up slightly to the left, aiming for a pair of bolts. From here, slant right up a downward-facing flake (beneath and right of a prominent right-facing corner). Some airy moves on slopers with your feet well above your gear completes this amazing experience. Belay at a ledge with a bolt.

Descend by scrambling onto the west face. It is necessary to traverse across a dicey and exposed slab (5.2) to reach the large ledge at the top of *West Overhang*. From this ledge, downclimb to a rappel station near the old dying rappel tree. You can also downclimb *The Bomb* (5.4) which is mostly in fourth class gullies.

3. The Rainbow Wall 5.13a

This route is easily found as it ascends the beautiful diamond shaped rainbow-colored wall facing South Boulder Creek. The often-tried route was first ascended as a free route by Bob Horan. Harrison Dekker almost bagged the second ascent, but was too pumped to hang on to the anchor quickdraw and took the big whip. Bring a #2 Friend for pro before the first bolt. Follow the bolt line up and left to a new two bolt anchor.

 Several options exist for descent possibilities for the **next several routes** on the west face. Except for the *Wind Ridge*, however, I can't recommend doing the final summit pitches for these climbs. It's best to just scramble off from the long ledge above the second pitches of these routes. If you do summit, descend by scrambling down a little to the east (where huge loops of cable lie) and continuing north until a notch with rappel anchors is reached. Make a short rappel from the bolt anchor. Beware of the loose rock. From here pick up the Redgarden Wall descent trail.

4. The Bomb 5.4

This is easiest way to the top and also a possible downclimb for *Metamorphosis*. Start from a ledge 20' from a large block and move up a right-facing corner. Continue up to a groove past a tree and onto another ledge. Go left to ascend a chimney, and belay on a ledge above a juniper tree. Move up to the south ridge, then continue up loose rock to the summit.

Wind Tower

5. West Overhang   5.7
Start in a slot on the right side of the aforementioned block. Ascend the slot followed by an easy chimney. When you reach the ledge in the middle of the face, step right (past *The Bomb's* chimney). The next pitch tackles the large inset roof and continues on easier ground to a large ledge. Rappel from bolts near the tree, as the summit pitch isn't any good.

6. Reggae   5.8
This route begins from the 2-bolt anchor at the first belay of Calypso, though it could be accessed via the first pitch of any of the previous routes. The route begins down and 10 feet right of the bolts. Start up the right-facing dihedral with some mini-roofs. A finger crack to a slot provides the crux of the route. When you get to the belay alcove, scour the area for tricky gear placements to provide a belay. Pay attention to solution pockets, one of which allows for a tunnel thread. Belay from a good stance here. Continue to the summit on easy terrain.

7. Calypso   5.6
Begin left of the large boulder and traverse into the large right-facing dihedral. This short section of easy face climbing is unprotected. The pitch ends at a bolted stance after a beautiful pitch of liebacking and underclinging. The second pitch jams up a steep 20' crack just up and left of the bolts past a fixed piton. Set up a belay on another nice ledge. Pitch 3 climbs a corner and then up to the summit.

8. Tagger   5.10b/c
An excellent first pitch (.9) pulls the obvious roof which is somewhat tricky to protect. Belay at bolts near a tree.

Though it is possible to make it over the crux roof from here, most people climb an easy pitch to anywhere beneath the crux roof where it is safe and comfortable to belay (.6).

The crux pitch pulls the large roof and continues to the walk-off ledge, though belaying at the lip makes communication easier.

9. Wind Ridge   5.6 or 5.8
This highly-recommended climb follows an airy line that forms the skyline of the Wind Tower when viewed from the bridge. Hike the trail to a cozy staging area where the belayer can escape the sun in the shade of a good sized tree.

You may choose from two options at the start of the climb. The first and easiest way goes left up a ramp (5.6) before traversing back right onto the ridge. The other option is to climb a large flake above the ledge and go straight up the ridge (5.8). The first pitch will deposit the leader on a recessed ledge where creative nut craft or camming devices provide anchors.

Traverse right along a small ledge until a crack shoots straight up. This pitch involves jams of different sizes from fingers to chimney. This pitch is best done as a fairly long lead (avoiding the temptation to belay at the first ledge with the single fixed pin). The best belay is set up on a long ledge beneath an imposing overhang. If you choose to, you can bail here by traversing left to the descent gully.

The final pitch, tackles the bizarre roof by a series of slithering moves that leads one to a butt-rest behind a hollow flake and then to a belay ledge slightly left of the summit. Descend as described on the previous page and be careful on the exposed scrambles, as some downclimbing is required to reach Ivy Baldwin's old tightrope cables.

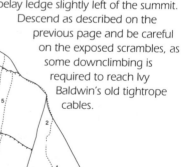

Whale's Tail

The Whale's Tail can be identified from across the creek as the 200' piece of rock with a cave. Routes are listed in a logical fashion as they are approached in a clockwise manner with sport routes, moderate cracks, and even a slab included. To get to the south face simply cross the bridge and hang a left at its end, walk 20' and, you'll find yourself in front of the Whale's Tail. A scramble north and east up talus brings you to the west face routes.

1. Free Speech 5.12a
The route actually begins on a 5.8 ramp *(Spoof)* that angles up and left (protected by pins and optional gear). *Free Speech* only climbs a short portion of this ramp before veering right passing two bolts. Initially the holds are river polished and slimy, but they give way to positive huecos.

2. M 5.10a/b
This route also first ascends the *Spoof* ramp (5.8). From the third pin on Spoof, move up right past a couple of bolts pulling the tricky roof. There is a 2- bolt belay.

3. The Monument 5.12c or 5.13a
Begin inside the cave and exit via chalked holds. A stick-clip is recommended as the crux occurs before the first bolt. The route remains difficult (although knee bars provide no-hands rests). Exiting the cave on the right makes the route 12c and requires a 3/4" TCU or a nut. As a result most sport climbers opt for the 13a finish on the left.

While a variety of sequences will work, the best beta for *The Monument* came from the very fit George Squibb. A pair of young children watching a climber near the third bolt asked, "How do you do that?" To which George responded, "You grab the biggest holds you can find and pull them down to your waist." The beta has seemingly universal application.

Ben Moon flashing The Monument 5.13a
Photo by Dan Hare

Whale's Tail

The following two routes require a 60 meter rope or double ropes to descend. The rappel anchor consists of swaged cable around a tunnel thread. Most people rappel to the starting ledge and scramble off, however two ropes get you all the way to the ground.

4. West Dihedral   5.4

A terrific pitch with some good pro located on the west side of the Whale's Tail. Approach from the gully to the left of the starting ledge and traverse right to the starting ledge, encountering a few 5th class balance moves. This route ascends the obvious left-facing dihedral on the right. Traverse over to *West Crack's* anchors to descend.

5. West Crack   5.2

Begin this stellar route from the same ledge as *West Dihedral*. Pass a bulge, and jam up the easy crack. Belay from the in-situ cable.

6. C'est What   5.11b/c R

To continue our tour of the Whale's Tail proceed in the clockwise direction around the structure. *C'est What* faces northwest and ascends the smooth overhanging wall just right of a large roof. The 5.8 slab which gains the bolted face can be protected by RP's and small wires but is still sporty. A #2 friend protects the first clip. Three bolts protect the hard climbing. Lower off from chain anchors.

7. Jack the Ripper   5.9+ R

This route begins as for *C'est What*, up the difficult to protect slab on the northwest face. From the slab move into a shallow corner with incipient cracks (crux). Traverse out under the roof (5.8 and difficult to protect at the start since the old piton fell out). From here either ascend the arete to the top or downclimb a little to the *C'est What* anchors to rappel off.

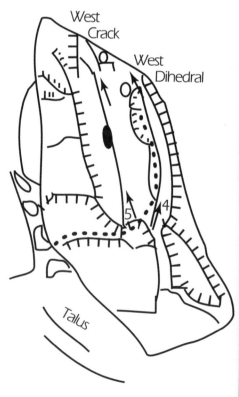

Redgarden Wall - Introduction

The Redgarden Wall is the massive wall which dominates Eldorado Canyon on the north side. Its sheer size and varying aspects make it a guidebook writer's worst nightmare to describe. Even photographs and topos play tricks as the walls, towers, and aretes take on a new shape with each step. We accept this challenge as you should not be denied such classics as *The Bulge, The Naked Edge, Ruper,* and the other routes covered in this guide.

Popular climbs exist on the east, south, and west faces of the Redgarden Wall. I have tried to introduce routes in the most logical way possible, in this case working in a clockwise direction starting at routes on the east side of the wall. Your first step should be to cross the bridge, head left passing the Monument Cave and ending up on the concrete slab. From here you can survey the vastness of the cliff, flip through the guide, and attempt to identify features and routes. You may also hear parties' futile attempts to communicate over the creek noise. Several trails, which will be discussed on an as-you-need-to-know basis branch from here and will take you to the various sides of the wall.

The *East Slabs Descent Route* is used for many climbs which end at the top of the wall. I do not recommend trying to find it in the late evening or dark.

East Slabs Descent Route: Scramble into the wooded gully just east of Tower Two, hike SE for 10', then climb up on the rib on the left when the gully drops away. Scramble down this rib to the south, move around a short overhang, then down a groove for 125'. Stem down past a bulge, then left into another groove, follow it for 100' or so. Now go to a grassy ledge with junipers on it. Step into a V-slot and down climb (4th class) to a gully between the East Slabs and a prominent ridge that cuts in from above and left (Hawk-Eagle Ridge). Find a footpath that leads you down past a chockstone to pick up the Wind Tower trail.

Tops of Towers 1 and 2

East Slab Descent Route

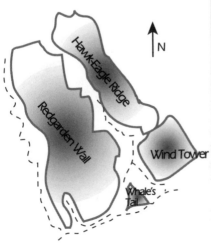

Redgarden - The Bulge Wall

To reach the Bulge Wall from the concrete block next to the creek, meander up boulders to a grassy bench above the Whale's Tail. Alternatively, approach from the Wind Tower trail.

1. The Bulge   5.7 R or 5.9 R

A high quality route up steep and spectacular terrain, with good protection at the crux. Nonetheless, a couple of funky and dangerous traverses can wig out the follower as well as the person on the sharp end.

Start from the east end of the saddle between the Whale's Tail and the eastern terminus of Redgarden Wall. Climb the path of least resistance to a small roof and left-facing dihedral protected by a pin (crux of first pitch). Pull up and run it out on 5.4 terrain to a bolt anchor.

Move up to a flake/undercling and jet right for about 15 feet, get in good directionals, then traverse left about 50 feet to a belay with fixed gear. (Dangerous for the second, although a #4 Camalot can provide a directional up and right of the belay).

The next pitch wanders up and right past a bolt and then left a few feet before ending at an uncomfortable belay stance.

From here one can escape via unprotected 5.6 climbing to the right or by climbing the short protectable 5.9 crack over a bulge. Head north to get to the descent route.

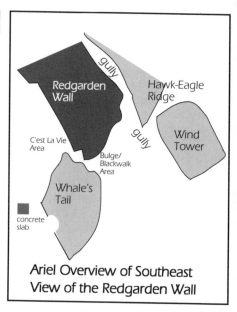

Ariel Overview of Southeast View of the Redgarden Wall

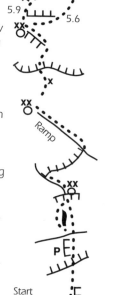

2. Backtalk   5.10c R

Start at a short left-facing corner found in the middle of the grassy bench, then climb up and right to an overlap. Step left a bit, then proceed straight up passing a bolt. Friends #1.5 and #2, a couple of bolts, and a half-driven LA bring you to a 2- bolt anchor. Rappel down.

3. Blackwalk   5.10b/c R

Begin as for *Backtalk* and ascend a left-facing corner up and right to an overlap. Zig back up and left to the first bolt at an undercling. Again moving left, pass two bolts and the crux. A 5.8 ramp will deposit you at a 2-bolt belay . Rap 100'.

4. Back in Black   5.11d/12a

Begin up a ramp left of #3. Place a #1.5 or #2 Friend to protect reaching the first bolt. Follow 7 bolts to a 2-bolt anchor (120'). Step left from this belay and continue 70' past 4 bolts to Fixe' ring anchors. Double rope rap or top out and walk down the East Slabs Descent.

Redgarden

Look up from the concrete slab and you're bound to see the ominous hanging dihedral on the south side of the Redgarden Wall. This dihedral, *C'est La Vie* is an obvious landmark, as is its steep left wall *Desdichado (13c)*. Scramble up the faint trail over boulders and bushes to the base.

5. C'est La Morte 5.9

Scramble up blocks at the base of the cliff beneath the *Desdichado* overhang and move about 25' to the right of the start of *C'est La Vie*. Climb an unprotected ramp up and left to an undercling (5.6 R), move up and right, then step into the cruxy thin crack. Rappel 80' from a two-bolt anchor.

6. Je T'aime 5.12c R

This sustained climb ascends *C'est La Morte* for the first 60'. When you get to a roof, branch left and make tricky moves to clip the first bolt. From here follow a line of least resistance that still allows you to clip the bolts. Same anchors and descent as for *C'est La Morte*.

7. C'est La Vie
5.9+ or 5.11b

Scramble up to a comfortable ledge 15' above the talus. Ascend a small crack that peters before another ledge. The crack protects well and even sports a bolt for further confidence. A shallow corner houses a bent soft iron pin (long sling helpful) which marks the start of the difficulties. A bolt protects a traverse move to an undercling (5.9+). Layback a flake to a two-bolt anchor.

Many parties set up a toprope and lower off from here, though the actual pitch continues up and left through a roof to a no hands rest. Above the roof, place a few small cams and make a

balancy step left (crux) to another two-bolt belay.

From here you have four options. If you fell repeatedly on the bent pin count your blessings and abseil. If the first pitch was enjoyable but challenging, try the 5.8+/9 crack right of the dihedral. If you need quite a bit more arousal, try the dihedral itself (5.11b). If you practically soloed the first pitch in your sandals, turn your eyes toward *Desdichado*.

Redgarden - The South Buttress

8. Desdichado 5.13c

Approach via the first pitch of *C'est La Vie*. Begin up the 5.11b corner pitch but shoot left along the massively overhanging wall following a line of four ring bolts. Turn the roof at the fourth bolt and keep it together until you reach a huge rest at the end. From here downclimb a bit and jump. Lower back to the *C'est La Vie* belay and one rap will get you down to the starting ledge.

9. Pansee Savage 5.11b R

A testament to technique and tenacity, this edgy slab route requires focus. As you scramble above the talus move to a ledge on the left of the *C'est La Vie* starting ledge. Start off the ledge and encounter balance moves right away. The three bolts are kindly located at the cruxes. At the third bolt, go right, then angle up and left aiming for the bolted *C'est La Vie* belay. This route can also be toproped after you do the first pitch of *C'est La Vie*.

Felicia Ennis on *C'est La Vie*'s first pitch.

10. Genesis 5.12d
(5.11 to first anchor)

A must-do if you're feeling up to a historically superb but difficult route. Begin on the boulders at the southern base of The Redgarden Wall. Start just left of *Pansee Savage* and move up a thin, left-facing corner to an A-shaped roof (5.8), where you must exit left with awkward and balancy moves (5.10d). Continue straight up the vertical face passing two bolts en route to a left-facing flake. A two bolt anchor will greet you. Several options exist here. Rappel 80' or face the 5.12 option. This alternative involves moving up past another bolt to a roof, and then right to a 2-bolt anchor. Rap 120' from here.

Offshoots of Genesis

11. Le Boomerang 5.11d

This route will keep you coming back for more. Longer than it looks, this route begins up *Genesis*. At the A-shaped roof move up and right to a bolt instead of branching left. Keep going until you get to the *C'est La Vie* belay. Rap from here. Gear needed for *Genesis* start.

12. Lakme 5.13b

Begin as for 10 &11, but this time at the roof branch right to bolts on a dead vertical arete. Continue up (placing a #4 Friend above the last bolt) to anchors that lie above *Desdichado*. A 165' rap will get you down. (9 QD's)

13. Exodus 5.11b/c

Begin up *Genesis*, but at the bottom of the flake climb out left to a pin and several bolts. Move around the leaning right-facing dihedral to a bolted belay. A 60 meter rope will get you down.

14. Book of Numbers 5.12a

The first pitch is a safe but exciting lead with mostly fixed gear, though this is best enjoyed as a toprope after doing *Exodus*. The second pitch is rarely done. See the photo overlay for location.

Redgarden

15. Redguard 5.8+ R

An Eldo classic that is not advised for a novice leader. Loose rock, sparse protection, and polished footing has made this route responsible for many ground falls. Rack to #3 Friend.

This route begins about 70' west of *Genesis* and just right of the bolted route, *The Contest.* Ascend the large dark colored shallow corner. After 70' feet traverse left 20' to a large platform with a two bolt anchor.

From here choose the rightmost of two cracks up and right to a grove/ramp. Pass a two bolt anchor (possible belay) and keep moving up the grove/ramp to a belay just below a huge black dihedral.

Lieback into the dihedral, then stem for about 100' to a belay stance on the left.

Continue to ascend the thinning ramp on the left wall for about a ropelength to a two tiered belay.

Continue up the ramp system to a cave belay.

The last pitch is intimidating as it works right up a vertical wall to a ledge. Next you want to start heading toward the groove between the South Buttress and Tower Two. To do this, traverse left into a groove and continue left around a large chockstone, and belay above.

Descend by scrambling northeast to the East Slabs Descent Route.

16. The Contest 5.12a

This mildly overhanging wall is found at the junction of the lower part of the Tower Two arete and the South Buttress. Begin this 80' climb just to the left of *Redguard.* If you're shorter than 5'9" you might consider stick-clipping the first bolt. (The first move is harder for shorties, but please don't "talk short" or whine, as it bothers those of us at average height.) Follow the series of bolts up and left to the arete, pulling a nail-biting crux after the fourth bolt. Pass the last bolt on the west side of the wall.

Redgarden - Tower Two

17. Touch and Go   5.9

A two pitch outing that begins in a puddle at the birth of the "Roof Routes" roof, which begins here and extends—continually getting higher— west across the south face of the Redgarden Wall. Continue north along the wall passing *The Contest* until you arrive at the roof, about ten feet above a wet spot.

Climb up to this roof and look for a tunnel thread a few moves into the traverse. Continue left, pull the roof, and step up into a crack/slot. Continue up the crack to a cramped belay (5.8+). (I've seen climbers deck on the first crux, thus I recommend slinging the tunnel for protection).

Pitch two ascends a shallow right-facing dihedral and predominantly protects with small wires and RP's— a stellar pitch.

 Two ropes make the descent less touch and go, as this allows a rappel from two Metolius bolts. Otherwise you must swing back to the slings below the dihedral or continue up the ramp (at the second belay) for about 60' to the *T2* rappels (one rope works for these).

18. Bolting for Glory   5.10a

A good alternative to the scarier second pitch of *Touch and Go*. At the sloping incut ramp halfway up *Touch and Go*, edge directly up a steep slab on sloping edges (5.10a) past 4 bolts to the double bolt belay ledge.

Two rope rap to the ground.

19. The Naked Edge   5.11b

First climbed in 1962 by Layton Kor and Bob Culp, the route has of course been freed, climbed nude, soloed by Derek Hersey, and is now on the cover of this book. If your ability permits and you have time to do only one route in Boulder, *The Edge* is it.

The Edge follows the left skyline of Tower Two as viewed from the concrete slab near The Whale's Tail. Look for the Lower Meadow, then let your eyes survey the skyline.

Several routes can be used to gain access to the route. *Rosy Crucifixion, Touch and Go,* or *T2* are my favorites. Another access route is to ascend *The Ramp* (5.2), a crawl-fest that starts at the base of *The Contest* and is usually soloed to *The Cave* (5.8)— unaesthetic but quick. Bring a rack with RP's, wired stoppers, and Friends to #4.

Begin at a bolted sloping belay ledge just above *The Cave* and beneath one of the most beautiful finger cracks ever created (in a very open book). Climb this 5.11a crack to a 2-bolt belay about 70' up.

The next pitch heads up the slabby arete, steps around the arete to the left where it gets steep, and follows a tricky-to-protect seam to an amazing belay (5.10c R).

A long 5.8 pitch heads up the arete for about 50' (gear to #3 Friend) to a mantle where you'll jot right and climb another 70' or so to a ramp beneath a chimney. Belay.

Climb this strenuous/weird bombay chimney (5.11b crux) for 60' to a hanging belay on the arete.

Bizarre moves take you through a shallow corner (5.11b), to the right side of the arete into a steep wide crack in a corner (5.11a). Belay at a ledge. Traverse to the left and you've done it.

Move northeast past trees along a sloping ledge to the middle of the East Slabs Descent Route.

20. T2 5.10d

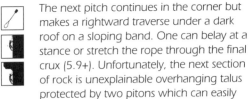

Suffering from an identity crisis for the last several years, *T2* stands for Tower Two. *T2* has mucho historical significance, as it was the first long hard free route up Tower Two. The drilled pin at the roof's lip was a rap job—a testimony to how ahead of the times Boulder ethics were.

T2 starts past *Touch and Go* at the first obvious weakness in the large part of the roof. Crank up to a drilled baby angle (crux with groundfall potential). Meander up past a variety of fixed gear (supplement with some of your own) and belay at a pair of bolts.

The next pitch heads up a shallow chimney 20' to the left of these bolts.

The third lead goes up a rotten red crack and traverses around a corner to a low spot on the Upper Meadow.

From the Upper Meadow, locate an ominous black groove to the right of the beautiful *T2* crack (about 70' uphill from the third pitch). Begin up this slot, then angle left on face holds past an antiquated pin or two until the phenomenal crack is reached (5.9).

This crack is followed to a tiny belay stance (5.8). Back cleaning or not protecting the initial part of the crack offers a better toprope for the second. While several stopping points offer belay possibilities, the first ledge is probably the most comfortable.

The next pitch continues in the corner but makes a rightward traverse under a dark roof on a sloping band. One can belay at a stance or stretch the rope through the final crux (5.9+). Unfortunately, the next section of rock is unexplainable overhanging talus protected by two pitons which can easily be wiggled by hand. My gut feeling is that it is best not to fall on this gear.

Two more pitches traverse upward and left on easy terrain, aiming for the notch in the saddle. Finish at the tree at the top of *Ruper*. From here, difficulties don't exceed 5.5 but protection is sparse.

 Descend via the East Slabs

Olaf Mitchell, 4th pitch of *The Naked Edge*. Photo by Dan Hare.

Redgarden - Tower Two

21. Jules Verne 5.11b R

Eldorado's most notorious mental testpiece. Both crux pitches are sporty, but the fourth takes the cake. Begin as for *T2* but traverse left along the lip of the roof. Make a difficult move (5.11a) to get established on a hollow flake, clip a very bad upside-down piton, and don't fall until good gear can be had. The route now traverses left under the obvious arch, then up the black streak past several 1/4" bolts. Set up a belay on a good ramp.

Beth Bennett on T2
Photo by Dan Hare

Pitches two and three can be combined as one very long pitch. Ascend the crack and corner system directly above the belay. The crux (5.9) occurs near the top where the corner begins to lean to the left and appears as an overhang (the real crux is dealing with the abundance of pigeon excrement). Belay in loose rock on The Meadow and be very careful not to dislodge the talus.

The notorious fourth pitch ascends the shallow right-facing dihedral just left of *The Naked Edge* (gained via a chimney/flake affair). Follow a small seam until it peters out just above a small roof. Place good gear—large nuts, #1 Friend, etc.— and begin climbing the thin face above. The first crux occurs about ten feet above your pro, but another crux appears just below the broken band. I'm told that one can get RP's in the seam after the first crux. I haven't placed them, but I have taken the whipper from the broken band. I didn't get hurt, but my belayer got bad rope burns on her hands (encouraging Trango USA to sponsor her with a new *Jaws* belay device). At the broken band traverse left to a belay stance (5.11a).

Climb up over a small roof in a corner, then angle up to a belay in the middle of the face (5.7). Next, climb straight up to a ledge just left of *The Edge's* 4th pitch (5.10d). Set up a belay. From here, 5.9 terrain leads to the summit.

 Descend via the East Slabs.

Redgarden- The Roof Routes

Some of the best climbing in Eldorado is concentrated here in an area aptly named The Roof Routes. The routes here are mostly typical Eldorado "sport climbs"—sport climbs if you bring up some supplemental gear and accept the challenge of possible ground falls on several of the climbs. From the cement slab take the lefthand trail, but at the next branch go right. These routes are located under a roof about 30' uphill from the previously described routes on the Redgarden Wall.

20. T2	5.10d R	28. Downpressor Man	5.12a
21. Jules Verne	5.11b R	29. Fire and Ice	5.12a
22. Clever Lever	5.12a/b	30. Psycho	5.12c/d
23. Private Idaho	5.11d/12a	31. Wasabe	5.12c
24. Kloeberdanz	5.13	32. Evangeline	5.11b/c
25. White Lies	5.13a	33. Temporary Like Achilles	5.10c R
26. Clear the Deck	5.11a	34. The Wisdom	5.11d
27. Guenese	5.11a	35. Le Toit	5.10d R

22. Clever Lever   5.12b?

This powerful climb begins about 50' to the left of *T2*. *Clever Lever* is the right of two routes that climb through the roof at this spot. This is also the site of John Bachar's famous solo fall. After the first bolt pull a crux move reaching a huge horn, sling the horn, stand up and move to the anchor and lower. *Clever Lever* is most often toproped after leading *Private Idaho*. Like many folks, I'm inclined to believe that holds have broken, making this quite a bit harder

23. Private Idaho   5.11d/12a

Climbs past two bolts out a roof to a single bolt anchor. Lower to the ground.

24. Kloeberdanz   5.11a R

20' left of *Private Idaho* below a double roof and a broken red corner, this route begins on the right-facing corner protected by one upward driven peg. Move right passing a bolt in the roof and pull the roof on jugs (height dependent at 5.11a). Rap 75' from the hanging belay. 2nd pitch is 5.10R and steep.

Redgarden - Roof Routes

25. White Lies 5.13a
From the end of the 1st pitch of *Kloeberdanz*, follow bolts out the roof arete then up the blank wall on the left side of the arete. This route is essentially a hard short boulder problem.

26. Clear the Deck 5.11a
Usually toproped from the *Guenese* anchors due to extremely sparse pro. Begin just right of *Guenese* taking a direct line and later joining that route out left.

27. Guenese 5.11a
Guenese is a freed aid route that offers brilliant climbing protected mostly by fixed gear. A pin and bolt protect a rightward traverse to a shallow roof. (A headlock under the roof provides a no hands rest while you dink in a small TCU or some wires). One more clip protects a crux move to a 2-bolt anchor. For the full pump continue through the roof, around the corner and up the dihedral to another 2-bolt anchor (5.11b).

28. Downpressor Man 5.12a
Downpressor Man, a well protected classic, continues straight up after the pin and bolt on *Guenese*. Three more bolts and many hard moves lead to anchors under the roof.

29. Fire and Ice 5.12a
Just to the left of *Downpressor* is *Fire and Ice*, the finest 30' of climbing anywhere. Three bolts protect this classic. The moves are interesting. The climbing is slightly scary but safe.

30. Psycho 5.11a or 5.12d
Found 25' left of *Fire and Ice* is this stellar climb. Begin at a short, sloping ramp and climb through the brown band to a small right-facing dihedral. From here stem right at a bolt then up to a pin. A final bolt protects a traverse to a belay out right. You can lower from here or attack the crux roof ending at a sling belay. (Most people snag the belay then down-jump the roof).

31. Wasabe 5.12c
Veering left at *Psycho's* first bolt puts the climber on *Wasabe*, a sport climb protected by ring bolts. Many parties opt to stop shy of the roof (5.11c), feeding their rope through the last two bolts instead. (This is a little tricky to rig without long slings to tie off on). The roof (5.12c) is fun and worth your while, but one must still down-jump to the ring bolts to descend.

32. Evangeline 5.11b/c
This route is excellent. Begin 10' left of *Psycho* and end at chain anchors. A #2 Friend protects a very easy move and really isn't necessary, but may be appreciated, as would a long runner on the first bolt. The route does continue out the roof 5.11b/c A1. Aid out the roof to some chain anchors. Continue up and right to a bolt, up and left past two bolts, and then left to a small roof (#1 Friend), then up and right to the *Psycho Slab*. A small rack w/ stoppers and #1,#2, #3 Friends useful.

33. Temporary Like Achilles 5.10c R
Climb up a flake (crux) 10' left of *Evangeline*. Move up and left along the rotten band, placing some cams, then turn the roof passing a couple bolts and a pin en route to a 2-bolt anchor. The big roof above, *Undertaker* (5.13d), has seen one free ascent by Ben Moon.

34. The Wisdom 5.11d R
Sketchy! Move up the Lower Ramp to the left of *Temporary...* about 45' until a diagonal roof is above and to the right of you. Ascend up and right beneath the roof (5.10 R), and then through a rotten band. Move right to a belay. Climb up and right clipping a bolt at the lip of a roof. Pull the roof (5.11b) and belay at a two bolts under another roof. The crux pitch is obvious from here as it follows the crack/corner system above the roof. Finishes by joining *Psycho Slab*.

35. Le Toit 5.10d R

Move 40' further up the ramp from *The Wisdom* to begin. Head up an obvious line of weakness to a belay on a ramp just beneath the large main roof. Climb through the roof following a shallow dihedral (passing some old pins and a new bolt). Belay above the roof at a ramp. Follow this ramp right for about 50' and then head up a series of short corners to the Upper Ramp.

Descent: From here, finish on an Upper Wall route such as *The Naked Edge, Ruper,* or *T2,* or descend the meadow to the *Naked Edge/T2 rappels.*

The author (sometime in the mid-80's) on Downpressor Man
Photo by Sharon Vaughan

Redgarden Wall showing approximate path of Ruper (37) and Super Slab (38).

Redgarden Wall

36. Rosy Crucifixion 5.10a
The name alone has me reaching for my chalkbag. This is perhaps the best 5.10 in Eldo, and certainly one of the most exciting. Bolts added around 1990 take much of the seriousness out of the first lead, but the incredible exposure still keeps both the leader and follower on edge.

Approach using the Lower Ramp, which begins at the base of the Roof Routes. From the top of the ramp cut east and down to a hanging gully with a precarious belay perch. Anchor the belayer, then begin by traversing right across a horizontal weakness, past some bolts to a belay in slings (or combine this with the next pitch).

Derek Hersey soloing Rosy Crucifixion
Photo by Dan Hare

Rosy Crucifixion

.9+

.9

.10

4th

Block

Ramp

The traditional second pitch heads up a beautiful finger crack with the crux of the pitch occurring just before a belay ledge with bolts.

The third pitch (or second, depending on what belays you chose) jets up to a bolt, then heads slightly right to a belay on slabs above The Meadow.

Your two options at this point are to either finish on an upper wall route (*The Edge, Ruper, T2...*), or descend The Meadow to *The Naked Edge/T2 rappels*.

37. Ruper 5.8

One of the very best routes in the canyon, *Ruper* ascends the entire south face of the Redgarden Wall. Begin by ascending the Lower Ramp, as detailed under *Rosy*.

At the top of the ramp climb blocky terrain to a left-facing corner (5.8), then move up a chimney until you reach a belay ledge.

Traverse downward to the notorious "Ruper Crack", which is protected by #4 Friends or larger. Many acquaintances have recounted stories about this crack involving stuck climbers, Crisco, and dish soap, but I can't seem to confirm them. Nevertheless, you might consider not inserting too much of your body into this wide crack. The Ruper Crack ends at a comfortable bolted belay.

The third pitch begins off the right side of the ledge, heads up an easy corner, makes a wild rightward traverse (the "Ruper Traverse") and exits to The Meadow via an easy corner.
From The Meadow descend via low-angle slabs to the gully part of The Meadow. Locate a huge cave, look to its right to find a beautiful crack/corner system (left-facing) that heads up to the right side of the saddle of Tower Two. Climb this crack for a long pitch with a cramped belay in a slopey cubbyhole with one fixed piton (160').

The next pitch heads up the crack and traverses under the large roof past pitons that can barely be trusted to support quickdraws. Continuing to traverse left puts the climber in position to attain the saddle (some horticulture protection exists on this pitch). Belay at the huge tree in the saddle (160').

Descend via the East Slabs Descent route. Description found at the beginning of the Redgarden Wall section.

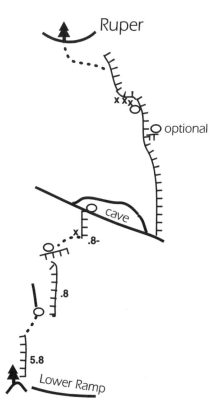

Ruper

cave

optional

.8-

.8

5.8

Lower Ramp

" I sell carabiners to rock climbers. But it's not as complicated as it sounds."

Ralph Imbrogno of Neptune Mountaineering when asked his profession at a Boulder art show.

Redgarden Wall

38. Super Slab   5.10d R

Super Slab is the prominent yellow slab formed by the juncture of the south and west faces of lower Redgarden Wall. When viewed from the road, this route is awe-inspiring.

Approach as for *Ruper,* but jot to the west along a ledge system. The route starts beneath fixed pins and a prominent undercling. It then traverses, following pins, to a narrow belay ledge beneath a prominent left-facing corner.

Climb pitch 2, the easy corner (5.6) for about 80′ and belay again.

Pitch 3 leads up then left into a blind corner with occasional fixed gear leading the way. Belay at a good stance, albeit airy, below a hanging corner system and prominent slab.

The last pitch climbs the colorful slab to the corner system (difficult to protect and the crux). Head up the corner, then over the roof to the top of the slab. This last pitch was formerly protected by a fixed piton which must have held one fall too many. Now RP's and LoweBalls can provide that false sense of security. (Actually, I've heard that the pin has mysteriously reappeared recently).

Descend by scrambling down the ramp to the 2 rappels below *The Naked Edge* or head north along the top of the ramp and locate slings around a large block. Make a 2-rope (165′) rap west to the base of the west wall. Another rap option is to find a ledge just below the ramp's west edge, and rap 150′ from a tree to a walk-off ledge or do 2 75′ rappels from the tree and anchors with one rope.

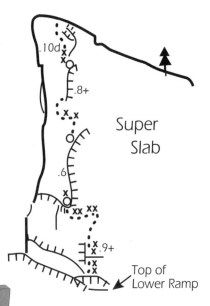

Super Slab

Top of Lower Ramp

"It's a slab dude. Your feet touch the rock."

Todd Eastman making fun of sport climbers and their insistence that steep walls are only steep if the biners don't touch the rock.

Redgarden Wall - West Face

We continue our tour of the massive Redgarden Wall by moving to the west face routes. To approach from the concrete slab, pick up the streamside trail heading west along the creek. Keep your eye out for a sign denoting the West Face Trail that meanders up the wide ravine below the west face.

Redgarden Wall - West Face

39. Suparete 5.11a/b
As you approach up the ravine and along the base of the west face, be on the lookout for a large Douglas Fir. Continue about 30' and look for a weakness right of a shallow dihedral with a piton (*Super Slab Direct Start 5.11c*). Climb a 5.4 start to a 5.2 slab (most people don't rope up) and establish a belay on a sloping ledge. Traverse left and follow bolts which can be supplemented with stoppers and TCU's.

From this point you can hook up with any of the routes leaving the Lower Ramp (*Rosy , Ruper, or Super Slab...*) or move to some rappel slings around a tree to the right.

40. Mr. Natural 5.8+
From the trail hike about 150' up the trail aiming for a buttress that bows out west. *Mr. Natural* begins on the right side of the buttress (south face) up a zig-zag crack, around a flake, and up to a ledge with a tree. This route does not hook up with upper routes. Rap 55' from a tree with slings

41. Vertigo 5.11b
About 150' up the trail you will pass the beginning of *Mr. Natural* and 180' above will be a very prominent dark right-facing dihedral. This dihedral provides the crux on the 3rd pitch of *Vertigo*. To get to the start of the climb walk past *Mr. Natural* and switchback up to a ledge. Backtrack along the ledge in the direction of *Mr. Natural/Vertigo* to the start of the climb.

Begin one of two ways (I recommend the rightmost): Either climb a wide 5.6 crack on the left of an unpronounced pillar or climb the out of view beautiful right-facing dihedral at the far end of the ledge (two pins 5.9).

Another short pitch (5.9) ascends a very awkward Eldoesque bulge/crack to a belay beneath the ominous *Vertigo Dihedral*.

Difficult moves off the belay lead up and left into an overhanging, right-facing dihedral with a few fixed pins. Pull up and left to a belay ledge. (The crux is really a boulder problem down low whose difficulty can be reduced via the long standing tradition of resting on the fixed hardware).

A fourth and final pitch climbs the steep 1" roof crack.

From the last belay walk north to a large tree on the Upper Ramp. Scramble down and right to a rappel station. Rap 80' or so to another rappel station. Another 80' rap deposits you on the Lower Ramp. From here walk down the way you approached.

42. Magic Carpet Ride 5.11d
Approach as for *Vertigo*. *Magic Carpet Ride* climbs the bolts left of *Vertigo* for one very long pitch to the bolt anchors above the 2nd pitch of *Vertigo*. Double rope rap or finish on *Vertigo*.

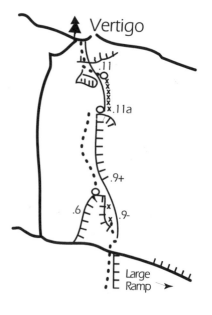

Vertigo

.11
.11a
.9+
.6   .9-
Large Ramp

43. The Yellow Spur 5.9 or 5.10b

This route offers a long, well-protected outing on perfect rock with amazing position and an awesome summit. Need I say more? Approach by hiking up the West Face Trail to a point at which the wall makes a large bend to the left (the *Grandmother's Challenge* buttress). Before reaching *Grandmother's Challenge*, look up at the yellow arete high above you—this is where you're heading! Scamper up to the upper of 2 ledges about 15' above the trail and about 100' right of a chimney in a corner. Bring gear from RP's to #3 Friends.

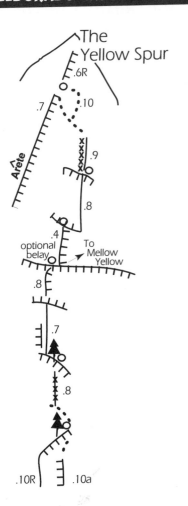

Two options exist for starting the *Spur*. A direct start begins in a crack/seam just right of a bolt route. This is mid-5.10 and tricky to protect. The more common start begins up a short right-facing dihedral 20' right of the aforementioned start. Head up this dihedral to a pin, then go left to a very short left-facing dihedral (another fixed pin is out of view). Continue straight up for 10', place directionals, and head right on easy ground to an obvious belay tree (10a).

The next pitch takes off to the left of the tree and follows an obvious right-facing dihedral past fixed pins (5.8).

The third pitch climbs cracks and corners to a slot and ends on a loose ledge. If you can set good directionals, you might consider belaying about 15' right (south) on this ledge to avoid the hassle of moving the belay.

The fourth pitch ascends a huge dihedral to a roof which is underclinged/face climbed to the right (5.8). Belay at a stance beneath and slightly left of the arete.

Now a fairly long pitch climbs the arete past pins and bolts to a belay stance (5.10). Belay at a stance beneath and slightly left of the arete.

The final pitch ascends the airy knife-edge arete to the summit.

To descend, follow the knife-edged ridge to the west (you may wish to belay) and arrive at a notch which houses a rappel anchor (slings around a tunnel thread). One rope and a short scramble will take you to a large rappel tree. Two more rappels put you on a ledge system that must be traversed to the north for approximately 35'. From another tree, rappel 75' to a hidden tree (perhaps not fully alive). A short rap from here takes you to the ground. Double ropes make this descent much faster.

Use your judgement, not mine, when choosing rappel anchors.

Redgarden Wall - West Face

44. The Great Zot 5.8+

Approach the same as for *The Yellow Spur*, but continue up the trail past the *Yellow's* start until you reach a deep chimney (the *West Chimney*) on the right. *The Great Zot* begins about 15' to the left of this feature.

Move up a shallow corner/thin crack up to a small cubby hole, jam the hand crack out the top of the hole (5.8), and climb the crack to a belay ledge (same ledge as for *Rewritten*).

A short, easy pitch up and right leads to a belay at the "Red Ledge" (5.0). For the 3rd pitch climb several shallow corners up to a roof, move left, pull over the roof at a left-facing dihedral (5.6), and continue straight up to another belay ledge.

There are many variations to the finish of the *Great Zot*, however, we have chosen the one that gives you the most bang for your buck. Technically called *The Zot Face*, it remains 5.8 but is a little spooky due to the exposure and the sustained moves. However, since our friend Karl led it, we think you can too.

Move off the belay ledge up and left to the top of a flake and then follow a crack another 15' or so to a small ledge. At this point the variation moves up and right (going straight up is 5.10) following a narrow ramp (5.5). Belay atop a flake at a small tree.

The next pitch steps right and climbs a dihedral to a face meeting several left-facing flakes. Angle up and left along a thin crack to a small, right-facing dihedral, move up the dihedral, and finally leftward to a belay ledge with a tree. The final bit climbs straight up to the ridge crest up an easy groove.

To descend from the ridge, scramble north to a notch, do some easy downclimbing west, then continue along the base of the wall heading south.

45. The Green Spur 5.9

It ranks right up there with its similarly named cousin, *Yellow Spur* and provides five pitches of outstanding quality. *The Green Spur* lies about 20' to the left of *The Great Zot* and about 15' of a prominent arete (the *Rewritten* arete).

Ascend a crack up the right side of a short pillar/pedestal, and belay below a chimney, 55' (5.4).

Tackle the awkward flare/pod (crux), which is protected by large gear, then find a crack which leads up to an overhanging right-facing corner. Climb this (sustained 5.9), step right to another crack, and follow this up to an eyebolt on the Red Ledge. Belay.

Move the belay 50' to the left along the Red Ledge. You will now be above *Grandmother's Challenge*. Ascend the block, up a crack, then crack a deceptive roof (solid 5.9), and continue up to a fantastic belay on the arete out left (*Rebuffat's Arete*).

Climb the rest of the arete, enjoyable 5.8. Step across and finish the climb on easy terrain to the top of the wall (5.5).

Same descent as for *The Great Zot*.

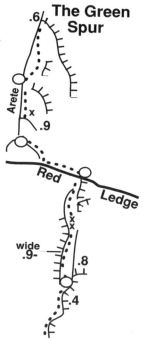

The Green Spur

46. Rewritten 5.7 or 5.8

As far as stellar moderates go, *Rewritten*, is nearly unmatched. This fantastic route begins in an alcove at the base of *West Chimney*, as mentioned in *The Great Zot* description.

Climb a ramp on the left, and gain a narrow ledge. Continue up a shallow corner until you reach a small roof next to the arete. Turn the roof, hand traverse to the right, then join a 5.7 crack that leads to a good belay ledge.

The next pitch climbs the chimney then face to the "Red Ledge" (5.4). Belay at the large eye bolt.

The 3rd pitch ascends the left-facing dihedral, then climbs a tight chimney. Belay in a pod above the chimney.

Make an exciting traverse left using a crack that bisects the wall. (exposed 5.6). Continue up a hand crack for 50'-60', and finish left at the top. Continue straight up the arete (5.8) or up a small corner on the right, and belay.

Continue with the arete and belay from slings around the summit. Stem over to a shallow dihedral and follow it to the top of the wall (5.5). Some larger gear is comforting on this route.

Descend as for *The Great Zot.*

47. Swanson Arete 5.5

This is one of my favorite climbs because it offers the novice leader or follower the chance to experience Eldo at its finest.

To reach the start of *Swanson Arete* you must climb the first pitch of *Rewritten*. From the belay, find the easy 5.0 traverse terrain to the right which leads to the top of *West Chimney*. Easy scrambling leads to the "Red Ledge."

Find the high point on the ledge (which happens to be behind a large tree), climb a left-facing dihedral to a belay at another tree (5.5).

Look for a nice crack system on the right side of the arete and follow it to a roof (5.5). Turn the roof (5.4) and belay on a nice ledge above.

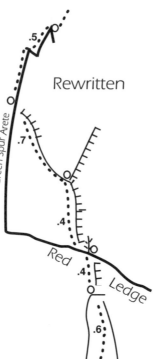

Rewritten

Green Spur Arete

Red Ledge

Now find another crack to the right of the arete, climb it to a roof, turn the roof, and ascend a good dihedral past a tree. Continue up a finger crack in another short corner all the way to the summit (5.3).

Descend by downclimbing to the south until you reach the saddle between Lumpe Tower and Tower One. Rappel to the west or take the East Slabs Descent route.

Redgarden Wall - West Face

48. Grandmother's Challenge   5.10c

Found about 10' left of *The Green Spur* this route begins up a wide 5.8 crack that ends at a chockstone belay. The difficulties begin as you struggle up an overhanging offwidth up to an impressive roof. Move to the right and lieback a flake up and over the lip. A final crack leads to the top of the face.

49. Darkness Till Dawn   10a

If you could look through the *Grandmother's Challenge* crack *Darkness Till Dawn* would be on the other side. *Darkness* is the prominent chalked corner.

Rap from the chain anchors. One 60 meter rope will leave you shy of the ground by about 5 meters. Easy downclimbing leads to the ground or for this reason you may want two ropes.

Heidi Knapp on
Darkness Till Dawn

The West Ridge

The West Ridge is a long intrusion running parallel to the west face of the Redgarden Wall. It practically blends with the West Ridge as you head west up the canyon. The ridge seems to rise straight out of South Boulder Creek and continues all the way to Rincon Wall. (Refer to the overview map for further clarification.)

Access to the West Ridge is very easy during late summer and fall as you can park at the Milton Boulder (see map) and ford the creek directly, ending up at the SE base of the ridge. During the high-water late spring and early summer months, you'll have to hike the Streambank Trail (which is accessed via the bridge near the Whale's Tail) all the way to the ridge. From there you can wade the shallow bank of the stream around to the SW face of the ridge, or scramble over a polished boulder. (Another bridge crossing the creek around the Milton Boulder is rumored to be in the plans; which may make this approach obsolete).

Once you are standing at the base of the ridge, an obvious path takes one up the length of the ridge, and into a less travelled and beautiful part of Eldorado.

We've chosen only a few of the routes on the West Ridge, but the whole area houses a great deal of quality climbing.

The West Ridge

1. Verschneidung 5.7

A classic Eldo moderate located on a section of the West Ridge called, appropriately enough, the Verschneidung Area (Arete Area). This area is located 50-60' above a giant boulder and a long dead pine tree. Also look for a flat slab with an obvious tree in the middle.

Start *VD* 80' above the large boulder at the left side of the aforementioned slab. Take a 5.4 corner on the right, or a 5.6 corner on the left (both right-facing) up to the edge of the slab. Head right and belay at the tree. Above and to your right is a very obvious V-slot. Climb this using a nice handcrack, and head left at the top.

 Walk off the back or rappel down the route

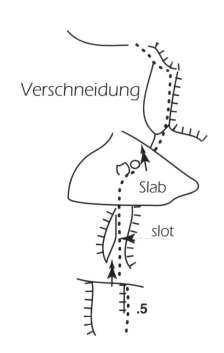

The Unsaid Wall as viewed from below

The Unsaid Wall

This area offers fantastic climbing, and is located just uphill from the VD area. This section of the ridge is easy to spot due to many very clean right-facing corners. A nice ledge cuts the lower part of the wall 30-40' off the ground, and is the starting point for the next few routes.

The best way off the following routes is to rappel 75' from an anchor near a large tree found at the top of *Washington Irving*.

2. Cruisin' for Burgers 5.10c

A great route found just left of *VD*. Start from the prominent ledge but move quickly into a right-facing crack with a detached flake. After pulling the crux at the end of the dihedral continue climbing leftward for another 50' to the ledge with the rappel tree.

3. Strawberry Shortcut 5.9+ R

Top off your Burger with a little dessert by moving to the climb just left of *Cruisin'...* Leave the talus by climbing a right-facing dihedral to a belay at an incut ledge. Ascend the dihedral, move up a slab to the base of a roof. Move up a left-facing corner, pull right above the roof, and link up with *Cruisin..* to the finish.

3. The Unsaid 5.9

Popular and classic—one of the best single pitch routes of its grade. Begin on top of a pedestal near a tree and leaning block on the big ledge. Ascend slabby terrain up to a crack in a shallow right-facing corner. Follow it to new rappel anchors at the top of the pitch.

4. Next to Nearly 5.9

A fun crack found between *The Unsaid* and *Washington Irving*.

5. Washington Irving 5.6

Classic moderate climbing that begins just to the left of the pedestal on *The Unsaid*. *Beware that the pro is pretty tricky!* Head up and slightly left and cruise the nice right-facing corner (5.5) which lies 15' left of *The Unsaid*. Turn a series of small bulges/roofs near the top of the dihedral (5.6), and belay from near the large tree.

6. Long John Wall 5.8

Hike uphill from *The Unsaid* for about 60'. *LJW* is the West Ridge's longest route, with five exceptional pitches of varied climbing up to the top of Long John Tower. Unique views of Eldorado Canyon are the reward. The only drawback to this (and other West Ridge routes) is the presence of poison ivy along the base of the wall. Long pants are a good idea for the approach hike! Gear up to a #4 Friend is advised.

LJW begins near a large tree in a poison ivy patch and climbs the face just right of a dark right-facing corner. Head left at the top, then back right into a crack (5.8 and a little spooky) to avoid a strenuous (10b) and runout roof band on the right. Continue up to a good belay ledge.

The second pitch ascends a nice crack (5.8) up to a roof, which can be turned on the left (5.7). Continue up the crack to a band of fractured rock, move left until under a slot, and belay.

The third lead cranks up the slot (5.6), then follows a right-facing dihedral up to a roof with good sized slots through it. Belay.

Climb the slot on the left, hard 5.8 and somewhat overhanging, and belay on a ledge after a short pitch. The final pitch tackles another clean slot straight above the belay, but the terrain is easier (5.5). Finish in a notch at the top of the tower.

Descend the east slabs of the West Ridge. Take care as recent mudslides have made the terrain less stable.

The Bastille

To find the Bastille look for hordes of people meandering about in the road and dodging tourist vehicles as they que up to get on classic lines. The Bastille is certainly one of Colorado's most famous crags, and contains possibly the most travelled route in the state, *The Bastille Crack*.

1. March of Dimes	5.10c	5. Outer Space	5.10b/c R
2. Werk Supp	5.9+	6. Wide Country	5.11a R
3. Northcutt Start	5.10d	7. XM	5.10c R
4. The Bastille Crack	5.8	8. The Northwest Corner	5.10c or 5.11a

1. March of Dimes   5.10c

The first pitch of this route is popular as Eldorado's only roadside toprope problem. The last pitch is often combined with *Werk Supp* for an excellent 3rd pitch.

Begin up a crack system left of *Werk Supp* that ends atop a small buttress, just above the 2-bolt toprope anchor. Pitch 2 climbs broken terrain to a dihedral, and up to a ledge atop *Werk Supp's* second pitch. The 3rd pitch takes on the left-trending thin crack. Belay from roots and clean gear.

 Gullies and scrambling to the east lead back to the road.

2. Werk Supp   5.9+

Begin pitch one right of a right-facing dihedral which forms the *March of Dimes* 1st pitch buttress. Climb up flakes and cracks to a left-facing dihedral which ends at a small roof. Step left (crux) to a bolt belay (150'). Move the belay up and left to the base of a beautiful hand crack w/ a pea pod flare at mid-height. Pitch 2 climbs this crack.

 Descend to the East or continue via *March of Dimes'* 3rd pitch.

3. Northcutt Start   5.10d

Most will find this stiff for the grade, but it's historically credited as Colorado's first 5.10, thus we won't upgrade it. Often toproped from the *Bastille Crack's* anchor, this line is also a fine lead.

Climb the left-facing corner system left of the *Bastille Crack* until a shallow right-trending crack allows a traverse right to the anchors on the Bastille Crack's first pitch. Rappel from the bolt anchor.

4. The Bastille Crack   5.8

The first ascent of *The Bastille Crack* occurred in 1955 and was accomplished by two US Army climbers: the free ascent was done by Allen Bergen and Stan Shepard two years later and was originally rated 5.6!

The route starts atop broken ledges and ascends a prominent flake until it is possible to step left into the crack proper. One can either belay at a small stance with a bolt and chain anchor, or the pitch can be stretched to the next ledge about 160' above the road. I recommend this method, though communication will be difficult. The section above the chains is a dramatic layback complete with nesting pigeons which love to startle unsuspecting climbers.

The next lead ascends a steep crack (5.7) past a fixed pin and ends in 40' atop a sloping ledge.

From here, move back (south) into a chimney/corner which can be ascended as one or two moderate (5.6-5.7) pitches to the summit.

 Descend by crossing a chasm to the south, then scramble up into a slot which is on the west side of the summit, and marked by large loops of old cable. Continue via a ledge system that runs to the south towards the railroad cut. Return via the new trail on the west side of the Bastille. Take care not to knock down rocks.

5. Outer Space   5.10b/c R

Start after doing the first two pitches of *The Bastille Crack* or begin after the 2nd pitch of *XM* depending on how you want to link. (Reaching this from *The Bastille Crack* involves an easy but scary traverse along a ramp before reaching the dihedral.) Climb a stellar left-facing always-chalked dihedral. Move right from the corner's top and belay beneath the undercling which marks the start of the next pitch.

The last pitch follows the undercling into a left-facing dihedral, splits left up a crack then up pockets to the top of the Bastille.

 Descend as for *The Bastille Crack*.

The Bastille

6. Wide Country   5.11a R-

Refer to the description for *The Direct North Face* link-up for the recommended pitch of this climb.

7. XM   5.10c R+

Follow a crack system that starts up a shallow dihedral and turns to hands, then into a chimney. Belay behind the pillar. Dink in small RP's and make a scary and somewhat dangerous traverse to the belay atop *Wide Country's* first pitch.

Continue up and left past 3 pitons, mantle onto a small ledge and move to a good belay. Again, not a good place to fall.

 You can rap with a 60 meter rope from the anchors on *Wide County* and end up atop a block 10' from the ground. From here scramble 5.2 terrain. However, almost everyone joins *Outer Space*.

8. The Northwest Corner   5.10c R or 5.11a

Begin left of the wide corner formed by the *XM* flake. Undercling up a slab and move into a crack on the right side of the XM pinnacle passing a couple of old pitons en route. Belay from bolts near the top of the pinnacle.

Next, climb over a small roof to a rounded weird crack near the arete. The exact number of fixed pieces varies as they often fall out. Head up this crack (5.11a) or traverse right to a scary mantle beneath a bolt (5.10c).

Pitch 3 climbs a crack and left-facing dihedral to a good belay ledge (5.8).

Pitch 4 is a short passage heading up and left under a roof to a long ramp. Traverse the ramp to the right and finish via the easy chimney of the west face routes

Descend as for the *Bastille Crack*.

The Direct North Face   5.11a R

This spectacular link-up, a combination of three routes —*Wide Country* to *XM* to *Outer Space*— provides a spectacular, clean, and direct line to the summit of the *Bastille*. The climbing remains consistently about 5.10 with a single move of 5.11 protected by a bolt. The route is steep and exhilarating with interesting moves as well as interesting protection. The second pitch, *XM*, sports a dangerous move, while the serious nature of the first pitch can be eliminated with crafty nutwork. A full set of RP's as well as a good selection of small camming devices is highly recommended.

Begin atop flakes and small ledges that gain a shallow left-facing corner. Ascend the corner (tricky pro) to a bolt and piton side by side. Move left (crux) and up to a sloping stance where you can recover composure. Next, veer up and left on unprotected terrain (5.9) to a small roof (5.10) which can be protected by 1" cams (long slings advisable). Head right around the roof to the safety of a two bolt belay.

Pitch 2 (*XM's* third pitch) ascends the leftmost weakness past three dubious fixed pins. The crux (5.10) occurs an unpleasant distance above the last of the pitons, and a fall might deposit the leader's ankles on the sloping shelf (but isn't excitement why we climb?). One can belay at a sloping ledge or combine this with the next pitch.

Pitch 3: Ascend the beautiful left-facing dihedral to a long ledge (5.10a). Set up a belay beneath a flake/roof.

Pitch 4:The final pitch (still *Outer Space*) leaves the comfortable perch and offers big exposure (5.10b). Climb out left via underclings, and ascend a left-facing corner past some fixed gear. Plan on dinking in some of your own. The corner gets shallower and terminates at a sloping ledge with a funky move. Traverse left until another weakness allows for an exit to the top. Belay just left of a giant boulder on the summit. Descend as for *The Bastille Crack*.

Pat Adams on Your Mother 5.12d
Photo by Dan Hare.

The Bastille

9. West Buttress	5.9+	14. Breakfast in Bed	5.8
10. Hair City	5.9 R	15. Out to Lunge	5.9
11. West Arete	5.8+	16. Sunset Boulevard	5.11c
12. West Chimney	5.7	17. Your Mother	5.12d
13. Blind Faith	5.10a	18. Neon Lights	5.11a R

9. West Buttress 5.9+

A varied route that offers a sampling of every sort of Eldo weirdness, this route begins low in the talus field on the west side of the Bastille. It essentially climbs the buttress thereabouts, hence the name.

The first pitch is identified by a traverse that wanders left through a dark strata of rock. This short 8' traverse places the leader at a vertical crack/seam. While this weakness can be followed straight up (more like mid-5.10), most parties opt to step left to easier terrain. Essentially, the goal of this pitch is to arrive, via the easiest path, at the base of the ominous large left-facing dihedral formed by the detached pillar of *Hair City*.

The second pitch ascends this wide crack past a bolt (crux). Thankfully, this bit is short, and one needs to enter the chimney system for only a short time. Belay atop the pillar at bolts.

Several possibilities exist for the next pitch, as one may ascend any of three cracks. The *West Buttress* proper ascends the leftmost crack system past a hard to spot piton and much pigeon residue. One may also exit via the *Hair City* or *West Arete* cracks, both slightly harder. Each of these pitches terminates at a large ledge system approximately 50' above the pillar.

An easy final pitch ascends a crack/chimney system on the left of the ledge. Descend via the standard Bastille descent described under *The Bastille Crack*.

10. Hair City 5.9+ R

Starting to the right of *The West Buttress*, this is perhaps the cleanest line on The Bastille, as it manages to avoid pigeon perches and wiggly holds (with the exception of 10' of suspended talus on the 2nd pitch.

As with many Eldorado routes, *Hair City* begins with a leftward traverse. The start is easily identified by a piton in a short right-facing corner about 30' up.

The pin protects the crux mantle. Continue past a bolt and into unprotected but easier (5.8) terrain. Wander slightly up past huecos and jugs toward the center of the pillar, placing pro under a small roof (long slings helpful). The easiest path from here is to traverse left (5.9) and head up on fairly good holds to the two bolt belay atop the pillar (also the anchor at the top of the second pitch on *West Buttress*).

The second pitch pulls a roof up the middle crack system (loose rock is encountered below the roof). Continue straight up to the belay ledge (pro slightly tricky) or traverse left to the *West Buttress* crack (locals won't let you get away with this act of cowardice).

Hook up with the final easy pitch of *The West Buttress* up the crack/chimney system on the left of the ledge.

The first pitch of Hair City

The Bastille

11. West Arete   5.8+

Originally dubbed *Duncan's Corner*, *The West Arete* has yet another creative route name. This route ascends, you guessed it, the arete on the west side of The Bastille. Approach by walking up the talus 30' past *Hair City*. Keep an eye out for a crack in the arete. The crack is gained by a leftward traverse and deposits one beneath the pillar mentioned in the previous route descriptions. A fixed piton and some slings serve as a belay anchor but could certainly be backed up.

A very short second pitch ascends the offwidth/chimney (5.7) to the top of the pillar.

The third pitch ascends the magnificent righthand crack, gained by a traverse under the roof. Unfortunately, one must navigate through pigeon droppings and levitating scree to gain this spectacular feature. Long slings come in handy on this lower bit, as they reduce rope drag and serve as protection around a thread/chockstone of sorts. Be conscious of your rope; though this pitch isn't a notorious rope catcher, I have seen ropes get wedged in the crack.

Finish the route as for the two previous climbs. Descend via standard Bastille descent described under *The Bastille Crack*.

12. West Chimney   5.7

From *West Arete* crack move uphill and follow the cliff contour as it begins to curve slightly east. *West Chimney* weaves in and out of its neighbor, *Blind Faith*. To start the route go up *BF's* wide crack. Climb this crack for 50', but bail up and left before the real difficulties start. Take refuge at a belay just below a right-facing dihedral which also has a wide crack. Climb this crack as well as the next left-facing dihedral. Keep an eye out for a good place to traverse right and clip a fixed pin. Switch back over to the chimney of *Blind Faith* at this point, and climb the big chimney to the summit. Descend as for #11.

"No I'm sorry, we don't have any; you might try Neptune's"

-Jimmy Cohen of The Boulder Mountaineer to a Denver newspaper reporter who asked to speak to a "traditionalist" during the Boulder Bolt War.

13. Blind Faith   5.10a

Approach as for *West Chimney* and start up the wide crack. Hang in there as the crack becomes tougher at its terminus 90' up. Belay at a ledge.

Pull through a broken overhang and into a chimney to the top of the route. Descend as for *The Bastille Crack*.

14. Breakfast in Bed   5.8

Approach by moving further uphill (40' from *Blind Faith*). *B in B* follows a very featured dihedral near an arete. Scramble up a ledge with a tree growing just north from where the route begins. Climb the steep left-facing dihedral staying right of the talus-quality rock.

The route ends on a ledge where you can scramble carefully around a bulge and continue south to hook up with the Bastille Trail.

15. Out to Lunge   5.9

Begin from the same ledge as for *Breakfast...* but slightly more south. Climb rightward until you encounter an awkward mantle that deposits you on a ledge. Climb the steep face, move left under a roof, and ascend the left-facing dihedral to the same walk-off ledge as *Breakfast...*

It's best to skip the second pitch and walk off after pitch one. Descend as for *The Bastille Crack*.

16. Sunset Boulevard 5.11c

This recently bolted route on the west face of the Bastille has become something of a classic de jour. Continue via the talus approach, passing *Blind Faith*, until a long expanse of slightly huecoed rock looms overhead. Surmount a roof that requires clean protection. The upper wall is bolted Eldo-style. This is a 140 foot pitch, without a fixed anchor, so prepare to walk off.

17. Your Mother 5.12d

Approach by heading up the descent route from the Bastille. *Your Mother* is the steep roof with bolts and chalk, clearly visible from the park bench on the Fowler Trail. Follow 7 bolts to a two bolt anchor.

For beta on sending *Your Mother*, see *The Monument* beta section.

To descend from the top of the summit tower scramble north, and turn west to the walk-off ledge.

18. Neon Lights 5.11a R

The pitch of *Neon Lights* worth doing starts on the descent ledge just right of *Your Mother*. Climb overhanging terrain in a crack system that angles up and right.

To descend from the top of the summit tower scramble north, and turn west to the walk-off ledge.

Rob Stanley on *Sunset Boulevard*

Photo by Dan Hare

Supremacy Rock

Drive up the canyon road to a picnic area right before the bridge and ranger station, you will notice a quartzite outcropping on the left. Several good routes are found on the overhanging southwest face.

1. Cold War 5.12c
Though it looks like you'll hit the ground if you fall before the third bolt, most people don't. Step right or hand traverse right at the top of the wall to the 2-bolt anchor located above *The Web*.

2. The Web 5.13b
Left of Supremacy crack is an overhanging, technical line of crimpers. Climb past four bolts to the 2-bolt chain anchor on top.

3. Supremacy Crack 5.11c
A fun overhanging handcrack that will challenge your tenacity and endurance (despite its meager lendth). Rappel or lower from *The Web's* anchors or scramble off the top.

Heidi Knapp on *Supremacy Crack 5.11c*
Photo by Dan Hare

"Four bolts on rappel or aid, and other techniques have created a web of the otherwise lovely, overhanging wall left of *Supremacy Crack*."

- quoted from HIGH OVER BOULDER

BOULDERING IN BOULDER

One of the greatest features of Boulder climbing is the abundance of excellent bouldering. Whether you want a quick fix or a remote foothills experience, it's here at your fingertips.

Lauren Chlebowski bouldering on Mount Sanitas
Photo by Dan Hare

Flagstaff Mountain

Flagstaff Mountain is the most popular bouldering area. Located above Boulder where Baseline Road heads up the mountain, the most frequented walls are found at a paved pullout about two miles from the "Fire Hazard" sign at the base of the mountain. Phillip Benningfield's *COLORADO BOULDERING*, provides exceptional detailed information on all the bouldering in the region and state.

Monkey Traverse

This popular endurance problem (waiting for your turn to get on the rock requires endurance) is found on the south side of the road, not far from the Crown Rock parking spot.

The Beer Barrel and The Slab

These boulders, located downhill from the *Monkey Traverse*, also offer excellent traverses as well as straight-up problems.

Red Wall

Across the road from the *Monkey Traverse* is the *Red Wall*, home of Flagstaff's best crimp problems, mostly V3-V6 in difficulty.

King Conqueror

Moving further up the trail from the *Red Wall* is *King Conqueror*, one of Flagstaff's best crack problems. A traverse also crosses the *KC* boulder, and a fantastic straight-up problem, *Face Out*, climbs crimps right of the crack.

Cloud Shadow Wall

A good choice on warmer days, this wall is best approached by parking on the road before the *Monkey Traverse* area at a small pinnacle —*The Capstan*—at a hairpin curve. The *Cloudshadow Wall* is downhill and east (across the street) of *The Capstan*. Cross a guardrail to find the approach trail.

An excellent traverse stays near the ground, and two harder problems exit either side of the wall. *Consideration* is the right hand problem, and is easier than *Hagen's Wall* on the leftmost end (V3+ and V4+ respectively).

Mount Sanitas

Sanitas is a great south facing crag offering excellent problems easier than those found on Flagstaff. Sanitas is approached via Mapleton Avenue, heading west from Broadway. Park just west of the hospital and take the western branch of the Mount Sanitas trail. A five minute steep hike leads to the beginning of the bouldering. Many excellent traverses line this beautiful trail, as do many beautiful people. As with Flagstaff, locals are happy to sandbag you.

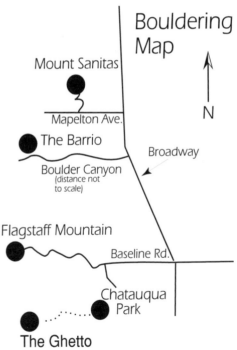

Bouldering Map

N

Mount Sanitas

Mapelton Ave.

The Barrio

Broadway

Boulder Canyon
(distance not to scale)

Flagstaff Mountain

Baseline Rd.

Chatauqua Park

The Ghetto

The Ghetto

The Ghetto was developed in the early 90's and offers steep bouldering in a remote (and tough to find) location. The approach is a beautiful 1.5 mile hike through the Flatiron trail system.

The hike starts at Chautauqua Park and starts up the wide Blue Bell Shelter Road. You will come to a fork at an outhouse. Do not go left of the outhouse down the Mesa Trail. Instead bear slightly right uphill. Before you pass a small shelter take a trail marked for Royal Arch.

Stay on Royal Arch trail about 0.75 mile. Along the way you will notice several raptor closure signs on the north side of the trail. Each of these signs correspond to social trails which all branch north. Just before the Royal Arch trail makes a major switchback south, one of these social trails veers north. Turn north on the social trail to a poison ivy choked gully heading west. This is followed to a point about abut 50 yards past a sport route *(Holier Than Thou, 5.11b)*. At this point you must clamber up a 15' high huecoed wall (10' east of where a tree abuts the wall). Once you get to the top, you will be looking down at *The Ghetto*.

The first area encountered (on the downhill end) offers short traverses and straight-up problems. Above this is a lengthy traverse along the lip of an overhang. At the downhill end of the traverse is a popular crack starting out of a hueco (V4). Many straight-up problems climb out of the dungeon—a chamber-like affair. All problems climbing out of the slot are long and difficult (V5+).

The Bario

Head up Boulder Canyon 10.8 mi to the *Nip and Tuck* crags (Nip is the boulder to the west and Tuck is to the east). Park near Tuck at a pullout by a picnic table on the south side of the road. Walk west past the roped climbing areas. Step over a guardrail and look for a long steep bouldering traverse. The entire traverse is generally considered V11, and many variations exist. It's almost exclusively upside-down climbing.

Bouldering on the steep roof of the Bario

Index of Routes and Crags

A

Ah Maw 5.10a 15
Aid Crack 5.10d 19
Android Powerpack 5.12d/13a 52
Animal Antagonism 5.13b 31
Animal Instinct 5.12b/c 30
Animal Magnetism 5.11c 31
Animal Riots Activist 5.11d/12a 30
Animal World 30
April Fools 5.11d 53
Archer 5.11a/b 54
Are We Not Men 5.7 21
Aretes, The 74
Athlete's Feet 5.11b 38
Atlas Shrugged 5.11d R 37
Aunt Jennifer's Tigers 5.10c 56
Auspice 5.11c R- 61

B

Baby Aliens 5.12a 21
Babyback 5.5 74
Back in Black 5.11d/12a 92
Back in Slacks 5.11b/c 54
Backtalk 5.10c R 92
Bad Sneakers 5.9+ 21
Bait , The 5.11a 32
Baker's Way 5.4 43
Barbarians 5.10b or 5.12b 33
Bario, The 126
Bastille Crack 5.8 115
Bastille, The 114
Batman 5.10 R 71
Bear Canyon 58
Bedrock 62
Beer Barrel 125
Between Dick and Ilga 5.12a 73
Bidoigt 5.9+ 57
Big Picture 5.12c 59
Big Spit 5.9 21
Black Crack 5.9+ 37
Blackwalk 5.10b/c R 92
Blessing in Dick's Eyes, A 5.10c X 73
Blind Faith 5.10a 120
Bolting for Glory 5.10a 96
Bomb, The 5.4 86
Book of Numbers 5.12a 94
Boulderado 29
Bowling Alley 26
Boys With Power Toys 5.12b 69
Breakfast in Bed 5.8 120
Brick Wall 18
Bubble, The 62
Bulge, The 5.7 R or 5.9 R 92
Bulge Wall 92
Bulgemaster 5.11c 73

C

Calypso 5.6 88
Direct North Face 5.11a R 116
Discipline 5.12a 56
Dome, The 17
Downpressor Man 5.12a 100
Drugs 5.11b/c 57
Dynamic Duel AO 34

Cannibas Sportiva 5.11a 30
Cardboard Cowboy 5.11 54
Castle Rock 35
Castles Made of Sand 5.11c/d 70
Cat-O-Nine Tails 5.12a 53
Catwoman 5.12d 34
Central Insecurity 5.12c/d 22
C'est La Morte 5.9 93
C'est La Vie 5.9+ or 5.11b 93
C'est What 5.11b/c 90
Chains of Love 5.12b/c 70
Chains Wall 70
Classic Finger Crack 5.9 15
Clay Wall 61
Clear the Deck 5.11a 100
Clever Lever 5.12b? 99
Cloud Shadow Wall 125
Cob Rock 19
Coffin Crack 5.10b 37
Cold Shot 5.11a 23
Cold Sweat 5.11d 62
Cold War 5.12c 122
Comeback Crack 5.10b/c 37
Comfortably Numb 5.12a 22
Coming Attraction 5.10a 60
Coney Island 32
Contest, The 5.12a 95
Cornucopia 5.13a 56
Cosmosis 5.10a 27
Country Club Crack 5.11b/c 38
Cozyhang 5.7 17
Crack 5.11 52
Crack System 5.8+ 61
Cracking the Code 5.11a 23
Crash Test Blondes 5.11c 23
Creampuff 5.12c/d 75
Crossfire 5.9 23
Cruel Shoes 5.9 21
Cruisin' for Burgers 5.10c 113
Curving Crack 5.9+ 37
Cussin' Crack 5.7 37

D

Dampened Enthusiasm 5.12a 32
Dan Hare Route 5.11d 21
Dan's New Route 5.11c 23
Dark Knight 5.11d 34
Darkness 'Till Dawn 10a 110
Days of Future Past 5.12a 30
Dementia 5.10a 21
Der Letzer Zug 5.12c 32
Der Reeperbahn 5.13b 32
Der Zerkle 53
Desdichado 5.13c 94
Devil Dogs 5.13 75
Diffraction 5.10a 86
Dinosaur Egg 60
Dinosaur Mountain 47
Direct East Face 5.6 R 43

E

East Crack 5.10a/b 19
East Face Left 5.5 R 45
East Ridge 5.10c R 79
East Slabs 5.5 17
East Slabs Descent Route 91
Easter Rock 33
Eat Cat Too 5.11 53
Ecstasy of the People 5.12d 22
Edgemaster 5.10d or 5.10b 73
Elanor 5.11c 34
Eldo of the People 5.12a 22
Electra Glide 5.8+ 26
ELEPHANT BUTTRESSES 14
Empire of the Fenceless 5.12a 33
Empor 5.7+ 19
Enchanted Forest 5.11b 60
Enema of the People 5.11d/12a 22
Enemy of the People 5.12b 22
Evangeline 5.11b/c 100
Evermore 5.12c 34
`Everpresent Lane 5.10d 71
Evolution Revolution 5.12b 30
Exile 5.12a 71
Exodus 5.11b/c 94
Extra Point 46

F

Face Route 5.11a R 19
Fact of a Doorframe 5.11b 56
False Gods, Real Men 5.10a 75
Father on Fire 5.10+ 54
Feeding the Beast 5.12a 30
Fern Canyon 63
Fertile Crescent 5.11a 70
Fiend, The 5.13c/d 61
Final Exam 5.11a 37
Final Solution 53
Fire 5.12c 62
Fire and Ice 5.12a 100
First Flatiron 42
Flagstaff Mountain 125
Flake 5.10 52
Flash Dihedral 5.8+ 15
Flatirons 39
Flies in the Soup 5.11c 32
Fluorescent Gray 5.11b/c 71
Fly Swatter 5.10c 32
Flying Beast 5.12d 34
Flytrap 5.11c 32
FM 5.11c 15
Fountain of Youth 5.10a 74
Free Speech 5.12a 89
Free Willie 5.11a/b 30
Friday's Folly 5.8 46
Fruity Pebbles 5.9- 66

G

Gagger 5.14a 32
Gap, The 71
Genesis 5.12d 94
Get Smart 5.10d 23
Ghetto, The 126
Gill Crack 5.11d/12a 37
Give the Dog a Bone 5.13a 32
Global Gorilla 5.11b/ 5.12b/ 5.12b 31

Gnome Wall 60
Goose Eggs 66
Goose, The 71
Grand Inquisitor 5.12a R 27
Grandmother's Challenge 5.10c 110
Great Race, The 5.9+ 21
Great Zot, The 5.8+ 108
Green Spur 5.9 108
Grins 5.9+ 21
Guenese 5.11a 100

H

Hair City 5.9 R 119
Hand 54
Hands of Destiny 5.12c 30
Hands Off 5.7 21
Happy Hour Crag 20
Haywire 5.9 74
Heartland 5.9+ 16
Hell in a Bucket 5.12d 29
Hiss and Spray 5.12a 53
Hot Flyer 5.11d/12a 23
Hot If You're Not 5.11d 53
Hot Spit 5.11c 62
Hot Wire 5.12b/c 23
Hound Dog 5.10d/11a 27
Houston's Crack 5.7 19

I

I, Robot 5.7 21
Ilga Grimpeur 5.11b 73
Ilga Slab, The 73
Iron Cross 5.11a 74

J

Jack the Ripper 5.9+ R 90
Jackson's Wall 5.6 37
Jackson's Wall Direct 5.10a 38
Jaycee's Dance 5.8+ 30
Jazz on the Mezzanine 5.12 a/b 29
Je T'aime 5.12c R 93
Jellystone Area 61
Joint Face, The 70
Joint Venture 5.11a 30
Joker 5.11b 34

Ruby Slipper 5.11a/b 75
Rude Welcome 5.11c 66
Ruper 5.8 103
Rush Hour 5.10b 21

S

Sanctuary 5.12 62
Saturday's Folly 5.8+ 46
School (of Primitive Behavior) 5.12c 75
Scraping By 5.10a 22
Screams Bunny 5.10 54
Sculpture, The 5.11c 61
Sea and the Mirror 5.10c 66
Security Risk 5.10a or 5.10d 22
Security Risk Crag 22
Sex 5.10c/d 57
Shark's Fin 54
Shoot to Thrill 5.12a 59
Skid Row 5.9+ 21
Slab, The 69
Slabmaster 5.11d 73

Snake Watching 5.13a 59
Sneak Preview 5.11b/c 60
South Face 5.10b 18
South Ridge 5.2 43
Spank the Dog 5.12b/c 56
Sporofight 5.11b 73
Standard Route 5.4 R 45
Standard Route 5.7 15
Standard Route, The 5.6 R 79
Sternadilemma 5.11d 70
Stoned Operation 5.11c/d 59
Strawberry Shortcut 5.9+ R 113
Suite 11 5.11c 29
Sundog 5.11d 30
Suparete 5.11a/b 106
Super Slab 5.10d R 104
Superfresh 5.12c 66
Superguide 5.9- 74
Supremacy Crack 5.11c 122
Supremacy Rock 122
Swanson Arete 5.5 109

T

T2 5.10d 97
Tagger 5.10b/c 88
Tell-Tale Heart 5.12b 33
Temporary Like Achilles 5.10c R 100
Third Flatiron 44
Thought Control 5.9+ 61
Thunderdome 5.12a 34
Tipsey 5.9 21
Tits Out for the Lads 5.12b 59
Tongo 5.11a R- 37
Toprope Arete 5.10c 71
Touch and Go 5.9 96
Touch Monkey 5.10d/11a 53
Tough Situation 5.9 15
Tower Two 96
Trail Routes 66
Tree Swing 5.8 52
Turmoil 5.11d 23
Twist and Shout 5.13b 32
Twofers 5.8 21
Twofers Gully 5.6 21

U

Undertow 5.12b 69
Unity 5.8+ 74
Unnamed 5.11d 59
Unnamed 5.12 56
Unsaid, The 5.9 113
Unsaid Wall 113

V

Variation 5.12b 79
Verschneidung 5.7 112
Vertigo 5.11b 106
Verve 5.13c/d 27
Violator 5.13c 75

W

Wagging the Nub 5.11d 34
Wall, The 61
Warm Up 5.10c 33
Wasabe 5.12c 100
Washington Irving 5.6 113

Juice 5.12d 23
Jules Verne 5.11b R 98
Just a Little Insecure 5.12a 23
Just Another Boy's Climb 5.11d/12a 69

K

Kent's Crack 5.12a 74
King Conqueror 125
Kloeberdanz 5.11a R 99
Knot Carrot 5.10d/11a 53
Kudjo Magnetism 5.12a 31
Kudjo Tranquilizer 5.12a 31

L

Lakme 5.13b 94
Last Call 5.9 21
Last Laugh 5.10c 21
Le Boomerang 5.11d 94
Le Toit 5.10d R 101
Left Crack 5.9+ 26, 27
Left Joint 5.10a 70
Left Wing 5.10b/c 15
Lieback 5.10a 26
Lightning Bolt Arete 5.12a 74
Liquid Crystal 5.11c 62
Living on the Edge 5.11b/c 18
Loading Zone 5.10d 32
Long John Wall 5.8 113
Love 5.12d 62
Love's Labor Lost 5th class 71

M

M 5.10a/b 89
Magic Carpet Ride 5.11d 106
Maiden, The 76
Malign 5.7 21
March of Dimes 5.10c 115
Maximum Security 5.9+ 22
Meals of Truman 5.11c 54
Megasauras 5.10d 62
Men are from Mars 5.11a/b 22
Mentor 5.12b 66
Merest Excrescences 5.12b 52
Metamorphosis 5.9+ R 86
Missing Link 5.12b 59
Monkey Traverse 125
Monodoigt 5.11b 55
Monster Woman 5.8+ 15
Monument, The 5.12c or 5.13a 89
Mount Sanitas 125
Mr. Natural 5.8+ 106

N

Naked Edge, The 5.11b 96
Nasty Boys 69
Nebel Horn 75
Neon Lights 5.11a R 121
New Beginnings 5.11c 31
New Saigon 5.11b/c 54

Next to Nearly 5.9 113
Night Vision 5.10b 19
Nightcap 5.8 21
North Arete 5.5 R 42
Northcutt Start 5.10d 115
Northwest Corner 5.10c R or 5.11a 116
Northwest Face 5.8+ 16
Nude Figures in a Hollow Fruit 5.11a or 5.10b 55

O

On the Contrary 5.11d 75
Out of Africa 5.13a 66
Out to Lunge 5.9 120
Outer Space 5.10b/c R 115
Owl 5.7 17

P

Pansee Savage 5.11b R 94
Penguin, The 5.12b 34
Perfect Kiss 5.11+ 54
Perfect Route 5.10c 18
Piles of Trials 5.12a/b 30
Pine Tree Route 5.4 - 5.5 15
Pitbull Prowser 5.11b 31
Plain or Peanut 5.11a 75
Plan B 5.12b 23
Polyester Leisure Suit 5.11a 37
Power Bacon 5.10- 66
Power Bulge 5.12c 54
Pretty Lady 5th class 71
Private Idaho 5.11d/12a 99
Prong 5.12c 32
Psycho 5.11a or 5.12d 100
Pup 5.9 23

Q

Q's 5.9+ 29
Quickie, A 5.11a 66
Quintet 5.10b/c 32

R

Rads for Rookies 5.8 75
Raging Bull 5.12c 71
Rain Shadow 5.12b 34
Rainbow Bridge 5.9- 75
Rainbow Wall 5.13a 86
Red Badger 5.11d 32
Red Wall 125
Redgarden Wall 91
Redguard 5.8+ R 95
Reggae 5.8 88
Regular Route 5.11b 26, 27
Rewritten 5.7 or 5.8 109
Riddler 5.11c 34
Right Joint 5.9- 70
Rip This Joint 5.10b- 70
Roof Routes 98
Rosy Crucifixion 5.10a 102

Web, The 5.13b 122
Werk Supp 5.9+ 115
West Arete 5.8+ 120
West Buttress 5.9+ 119
West Chimney 5.7 120
West Crack 5.2 90
West Crack 5.9+ 27
West Dihedral 5.4 90
West Face 5.9+ 27
West Overhang, Maiden 5.11b 79
West Overhang, Wind Tower 5.7 88
West Ridge 111
Whale's Tail 89
What If You're Not? 5.8 53
What's Up? 5.10a/b 15
Whipping Post 5.11d 69
White Lies 5.13a 100
White Man Can't Jump 5.12a 34
Wide Country 5.11a R- 116
Wild Horses 5.13a? 71
Willard 5.11c 34
Wind Tower 86
Wing Ding Ding-a-ling Down She Goes 5.11b or 5.9 53
Wingtip 5.10c/d 15
Wisdom, The 5.11d R 100
Work It On Out 5.12d 32

X

XM 5.10c R+ 116

Y

Yellow Christ 5.12b 52
Yellow Spur, The 5.9 or 5.10b 107
Yellow Traverse 86
Your Mother 5.12d 121

Z

Zolar Czakl 5.10a 16

I